How Ordinary People Make an Extraordinary Amount of Money Online - Affiliate Marketing, Anyone?

101 World Class Expert Facts, Hints, Tips and Advice

on Affiliate Revenue

Information is power – you know that. But, how do you research the best Affiliate Revenue strategies, without spending too much of your time (and money) on it? The average person earns $ 1100 per week, which equates to $ 27 per hour. Trying to do the research yourself would take you at least 5 hours to come up with the best information, AND you'll have to do this on a regular basis to come up with the most up to date and current information.

There has to be a different way to find the info you want! Well, yes there is... we did all the research for you, combed through all the information and got down to the hard core of the 101 most up to date and best Facts, Hints, Tips and Advice here, in this book.

The 101 of the most current, most actual and beneficial Facts, Hints, Tips and Advice you can find from experts in the field on Affiliate Revenue:

Table of Contents

How to Make Money With Affiliate Programs in Easy to Follow Steps....13

How to Make Money Surfing the Internet in 5 Easy Steps....15

Another Way to Double the Profits of a Website Using Chitika...16

Residual Income Affiliate Programs - Is Cheaper Better?....18

Proven Secrets to Make Money Promoting As an Internet Affiliate....19

Easy Ways to Make Money on the Internet - How You Can Earn Thousands a Month!....21

Learn Affiliate Marketing Today - How I Finally Did It....23

Internet Home Jobs....24

Affiliate Marketing - 3 Fast Money Maker For New Affiliates....25

5 Ways to Get That First Affiliate Marketing Check....29

Money Through Affiliate Marketing - The Truth About Making it Work For You....33

How to Turn Your Hobby Into a Paycheque....34

4 Key Strategies to Making Money Online With Affiliate Marketing With Little Or No Money....36

7 Key Steps to Affiliate Marketing Success....38

Who Do You Believe?....41

3 Tips to Help Every Affiliate Survive....42

Make Money on Internet in Just a Few Visits With Visitbank!....44

Affiliate Commission - Dumping the Beliefs That Are Holding You Back 46
Affiliate Marketing Programs - The Gift of the Recession 48
Affiliate Internet Marketing - The Importance of a Well Formed Goal 49
Tips on Affiliate Referrals 51
Affiliate Marketing Online Program - Making Money From Home Could Not Be Easier 53
Affiliate Marketing - The Psychology of Wealth 55
How Can I Earn Money? Affiliate Marketing Programs 56
How to Make Money on the Internet - Visitbank Products 58
Make a Small Fortune As a Visitbank Affiliate 59
Make Money Online - 6 Reasons Why You Should Start an Affiliate Marketing Business 61
What Public Speakers Need to Know About Affiliate Links 64
Increasing Your Affiliate Referrals 66
Affiliate Marketing - Take it to the Second Level 68
The Positives of Being Taught Internet Marketing by a Mentor .. 69
Why Do Publishers Join Affiliate Networks? 71
Building an Affiliate Marketing Website From Scratch 72
Affiliate Marketing 101 (the Basics) 74
Building a Residual Income Using Affiliate Programs 76
Affiliate Marketing Tips - How to Select a Good Visitbank Product 78

3 Affiliate Marketing Strategies - Do Something Today! 79
Earn $1000's in Residual Income Every Month With Global Domains International 81
6 Free Methods to Getting Insane Amounts of Traffic to Your Affiliate Program 83
Bills Piling Up and Money Just Doesn't Go Far Enough? You Can Change That Today! 86
How to Make a Lot of Money by Affiliate Marketing Fast 88
The Newbie Workbook Review - A New Marketer's Dream Come True! 89
My Online Income System - A Plan That Works 90
The Super Affiliate Home Business Model 93
What is Affiliate Marketing and How Can I Earn a Living at It? ..95
Affiliate Marketing 101 - Try Free Affiliate Marketing Before You Pay Google Or Yahoo For PPC 96
My Online Income System For You 99
What to Look For in an Affiliate Program Before Joining One....100
7 Things to Consider in Selecting the Right Affiliate Products to Promote 102
3 Reasons Why You Need to Cloak Your Affiliate Link 105
How to Launch Your Own Successful Affiliate Program 107
Easy Money to Make - Uncover the Secret to Affiliate Marketing Part 2 of 3 109
Make Money As a College Student 110

Affiliate Funnel System Review - Is Affiliate Funnel System a Scam? 111
How Ordinary People Make an Extraordinary Amount of Money Online - Affiliate Marketing, Anyone? 113
How to Succeed in Casino Affiliate Marketing 114
Affiliate Marketing Tips - 5 Tips to Promote Your Affiliate Links For Quick-Fire Profits 116
Affiliate Marketing Secrets - 3 Tactics to Boost Your Affiliate Commissions Almost Overnight 117
Make Money Online With Affiliate Programs - Getting Started 119
Affiliate Marketing Programs - The New Internet Economy 120
The Two Tiers of Affiliate Marketing 121
The Incredible Way to Start an Internet Business 122
Using Affiliate Programs to Make Money Online 124
Know the Character of Your Potential JV Partner 126
How to Increase Affiliate Sales Overnight 128
Warning - Affiliate Marketing Newbies! 129
Make Money Online on Autopilot - Discover 5 Surefire Ways to an Automated Income Online 131
Safe Work at Home - Affiliate Marketing is an Option 134
3 Things You Must Realize - Create Your Affiliate Marketing Mindset 135
Your Visitbank Profit Guide 137

Maverick Money Maker - Why Are 'Mavericks' Achieving Financial Success? 139
Affiliate Marketing (Why Do it) 141
Offline AdWords For Affiliates 142
Bob Proctor and His Affiliate Programs 144
Affiliate Businesses 146
How Effective is Wealthy Affiliate? 148
The Fastest Way to Make Huge Visitbank Profits 150
Affiliate Marketing Tips - How to Choose Affiliate Programs That Will Fatten Your Wallet 151
3 Steps to Internet Marketing - Free Internet Marketing Strategy 152
Why Affiliate Marketing Can 'Kill' Your Bills and Expenses Every Month 154
Make Money Online - Affiliate Marketing 155
Affiliate Marketing Tips - It's D-Day in Affiliate Marketing 157
Instant Cash Affiliate Programs - Making Fast Money Online 159
Affiliate Marketing Online Program - Stay on Top by Joining a Network 160
Learn Affiliate Marketing - Persistence is the Key 162
Affiliate Internet Marketing - Getting Past the First Month of Affiliate Sales 163
Online Affiliate Marketing Programs - Find the Program That Perfectly Fits With You 164

Ways to Make Money During the Recession 165
How to Make a Good Living Online.. 166
Affiliate Marketing Business Success in 3 Steps 168
Getting Started in the Affiliate Marketing Business 169
How to Fight the Downward Recession Graph by Working Online 170
How to Make Extra Money Once You've Retired 171
Money Making Machine - With Affiliate Marketing, Even a Baby Can Count in Millions 173
Are You Curious About What is the Easiest Affiliate Marketing Method? 175
Recession Trends - Make Money Online During This Recession 176
Some Points to Boost Your Affiliate Marketing Business 177
Recession Cycle - Can We Make Money Through the Recession? 178
Success at Affiliate Marketing - Is it Attainable? 180
Affiliate Mistakes - How to Avoid Them? 181
Successful Affiliate Marketing Businesses 183

How to Make Money With Affiliate Programs in Easy to Follow Steps

Affiliate program is the promotion of other people's products online in return for some percentage of the profit they make from the product you are promoting. Firms are not in need of a department made exclusively to take care of advertisement. This is due to they would have invested thousands of dollars or even more on insurance, tax, payroll and others. Due to this, they decide to own an account with reliable affiliate programs for the sole purpose of advertising their products for them. In case you don't know what an affiliate program is all about, it is simply a method of promoting the product of other people in return for a percentage of sales generated by you.

Some of the online stores that have affiliate programs which you can promote without any set up or upfront fees are Amazon, eBay, bestbuy, arts and visitbank etc. I am going to talk about how you can market affiliate products using visitbank, all others can wait for now. Visitbank gives you free access to register with them as a marketer. They have thousands of products which you can market via online. The thing with visitbank is that they have only digital products meaning you only get to promote software and e-books. You can select from the thousands of products by surfing through their marketplace. When you have found the product of your choice, simply create a hoplink and begin promoting their product with the link provided for you. There are varieties of ways which you can use to market visitbank products in return for a commission when you make a sale. Some of them are at forums, blog, your own website etc,

This is how it works. When you send someone to a merchant's page through your unique affiliate link, if they buy whatever the merchant is selling, you simply receive a commission. The commission you receive varies depending on the commission set by the merchant. It ranges from $15 to $100 per sale. Think of how much you would have made if you were promoting a product that offers $100 per sale, if you make 10 sales in a day you have made $1000 in just a day. Very fantastic, isn't it? Another interesting thing is that some firms run a membership program, meaning that for any visitor that continues to identify with them, they will have to pay a recurring fee. If you were luck to recruit a customer to one of these, it means you will be earning a monthly income regardless of whether you make any effort or not.

Most affiliate companies pay though check, paypal, ACH or wire transfer weekly or monthly. They are two methods to use for promoting affiliate programs. You have the option to promote their products through free or paid methods. Free advertisement needs much work, much time and in return you make sales, such free traffic as blogging and website creation. But paid advertisements like ppc requires much strategies, little work and sales. Less I forget, if you are not very good at ppc you will lose lot money without even making a penny through it. I recommend you spend a lot of time learning how it works and how to milk the best out of it. I suggest you join an online money making program where you can learn how to promote with affiliate programs successfully including ways to market. This is the best ways for a newbie to succeed, unless you would spend all your time trying to make money from affiliate programs without even making a penny.

Maverick Money Makers <http://modospot.com/review/maverickmoneymakers.html> is an online money making club dedicated to guiding people like you in the right direction towards making at least $250 per day as a beginner. It will teach you all the things you need to know to successfully make money for yourself online starting from now.

See more about it at http://modospot.com/review/maverickmoneymakers.html

How to Make Money Surfing the Internet in 5 Easy Steps

It is not all that hard to build a stream of income marketing affiliate products by surfing the internet. One of the ways to make money surfing the internet is through affiliate programs. Below are 5 of the most effective guide I have outlined and described so you can learn the proven way to make the best out of affiliate programs and most especially when it comes to making money from it.

Discover an affiliate program

You should begin by looking for an affiliate program which will match your way of marketing. All over the internet you can find networks of affiliate programs to select from. Make a proper selection by choosing from the ones that have a payment method that you will be comfortable with. Make use of the search engine which will show you thousands of affiliate programs where you can make a selection. Bear in mind that affiliate programs can also come in form of associate, referral, or even partner program. Step one of how to make money surfing the internet covered.

Register with them

Joining a referral program is an easy step which anyone can do. After you've signed up, you will be provided with a unique id, which is in form of link. It is through the link you will be connecting to people to the company's website. Most affiliate programs are free to join and it doesn't require any fee of any such.

Market to a targeted audience

After you've registered with an associate program, you should start marketing their product in a targeted manner. Do not promote a television set to people looking for PS 3. If you have a blog or website that is about the review of different TV sets or just talks about it, then you could as well place banners for tv ads on your site. Advertising in a targeted manner is the best way to succeed with affiliate programs. No matter the method you chose to advertise make it targeted.

Make your site Informative

Fill your website with all the guides your readers' need in order not to opt to another website to find them. If your website is a review site, try to include as much stuff as you can concern that your product. Promoting to a targeted audience will make you money surfing the internet.

Promote high gravity product

Do not promote products that are inferior. Promote products you know your audience will be willing to patronize and don't waste your time on junk products. If you promote a product for sometime and is not making you money, drop that product and promote other ones that are profitable. Now, let us say you have gotten a bit tip on how to make money surfing the internet.

Maverick Money Makers <http://modospot.com/review/maverickmoneymakers.html> is an online money making club dedicated to guiding people like you in the right direction towards making at least $250 per day as a beginner. It will teach you all the things you need to know to successfully make money for yourself online starting from now.

See more about it at http://modospot.com/review/maverickmoneymakers.html

Another Way to Double the Profits of a Website Using Chitika

The website you built for your personal use can be also turned into a money maker by using certain programs like Chitika. When you make a website that's going to make money you should know that Chitika is one way to double the money. If you plan on using Chitika, you should know how it works first. The chitika is one way to make the best out of the potential of your website.

The websites that you make can have both affiliated programs and Google AdSense. This means you can add the Chitika programs on your websites as well. The Chitika is a program that pays you for the pay per visit. This means they give you ads to put on your website for people to visit to get you money.

There are many websites that use the Chitika and other programs to make money, which will equal success. This means you will see a large amount of visits on your websites and also have more hits to it. This makes the websites in the search engine on the top searches. If you plan on finding a website that makes large amounts of profit by using the Chitika, then you should find a website maker. There are a lot of people that use the new program Chitika for their webpage to make more money. If you find a webpage that's for sell using all the AdSense, affiliated programs, and Chitika then you know it's ready to make you money.

There are many ways to making money on the Internet and one is through Chitika. If you use the Chitika you will notice its one program that makes it easy for signing up and putting it on the website you're using. The Chitika can be found through more ways than one and that's finding their website on a search engines.

They have many great reviews and as there are many pros, you are also going to come across some cons. This means you will find out everything you need to know about Chitika. The Chitika is one way to make your profits on your websites go up double the amount. The pay per visit allows you to make money when others visit on the Ads. The Ads can be any related items or websites that's being advertised. This means you can find an ad that's going to relate to your website. When you find a website that has ads, you should visit through those ads in order for the web host to make money.

Here is some information that can be useful for you and it's found in this Chitika review <http://www.duoblogger.com/chitika-review/> .

Residual Income Affiliate Programs - Is Cheaper Better?

There are many different residual income business opportunities out there and I have seen a lot over the recent months being promoted on the high price range. What I mean by this is that they cost thousands for you to join and I simply don't agree with it. I believe that if you want to promote something you should promote it to the general public and most people can't afford high-priced items in the first place. That's why I love to promote something that's actually affordable for everyone.

You have to understand that when people promote a high-priced product in turn, high-priced commissions is paid to them as well. For example if you sell a product that is $10,000, there's a good chance that commission will be close to half of that. That is a $5000 paid in one day so you can see why they're so popular.

I suggest if you are new to the industry do not take this route. You still have to get your feet wet and it is very beneficial to start learning with a low-priced item instead. I have been on the internet for many years now and I continue to promote things that are not high-priced because I want everyone to be able to benefit from it.

I am not saying that promoting something high is not right, it's just a strategy that has not worked for me and I know a lot of people who have been burnt from it as well.

No matter what you decide to promote just make sure you give it all you got and continue to strive for excellence. There will be times when things may not seem easy and you have to keep going forward with your eyes on the prize. The internet is a great business always remember that.

Want to learn how to make a part time income or full time living online from a measly $10 biz? Check out the link below to learn how you can make that happen.

===> http://www.MyMlmMagic.info <http://mymlmmagic.info>

Omar Negron is a 21 year old internet entrepreneur who is revolutionizing the way most people make money today. He teaches his simple residual income affiliate programs <http://mymlmmagic.info> technique that anyone can use to put extra cash in their pockets from their homes.

Proven Secrets to Make Money Promoting As an Internet Affiliate

Making money on the Internet has become so prevalent in the last few years, making "Average Joes" the new popular multi-millionaires. In fact, due to the current U.S. economy, a record number of individuals are flocking to the internet, out of financial desperation, to get a piece of the millionaire pie.

The common thought is, "if the average Joe can become infinitely successful, so can I." The problem occurs when these average Joes turned "Internet Gurus" begin selling their ideas on how to make money online.

Individuals who buy these guru products start out feeling like they're on top of the highest mountain with all of the hype stitched into the first pages of the product website promising internet wealth. But when the actual "training" begins, the millionaire hopeful is left feeling overwhelmed, confused, and incomplete.

This is because most programs only sell pieces of the puzzle, almost always insuring failure and disappointment on the part of the millionaire hopeful. With so many missing links, there is no way to attain the level of financial freedom promised with purchase of the product.

Unlocking the 3 promoting secrets of successful Internet affiliates is crucial. First, you must know what to promote. Second, you must know where to promote. Third, you must know how to promote.

In order to know what to promote, you must have invaluable resources available to you such as MILLNIC media. Just go to Google and do a keyword search. Check out the campaigns available to see what affiliates are making when they promote particular products.

Pay close attention to products that have free trial offers as these tend to get many leads. Another successful product that produces many leads are ringtones. This is because you don't have to have a credit card, be at least 21 years of age, or give out any personal information. Customers need only submit their cell phone numbers in which they will receive a pin number via text that they will have to confirm. Once confirmed, the affiliate is immediately paid for that lead.

Knowing where to promote a product is all about knowing the demographics of your customers. For ringtones, teenagers are your best customers. You can promote your product on Google AdWords by setting up a free account.

Instead of promoting on the search engine like most affiliates do through pay per visit sponsored links, why not promote on popular ringtone websites where customers are already looking for songs to download? Remember that people go to search engines to find websites they like, not to browse sponsored links.

Finally, knowing how to promote is simply creating your ad that will be on the ringtone websites. An example of a ringtone ad would read:

Latest Music Ringtones
Over 250,000+ To Choose From
Instant Download, No CC Required
(display URL here)

Did you find this article helpful? Then take a look at proven ways that take less than a week to get more traffic to your website which turn into more sales for you! Visit http://www.WebsicknessRx.com

Easy Ways to Make Money on the Internet - How You Can Earn Thousands a Month!

Looking for easy ways to make money on the internet? Are you wondering how thousands of people are making $1000s a day? Or even $500 a day? I use to wonder that too. Sitting in my room reading peoples success stories over and over again, how the internet has changed their life. Honestly you can read all you want but that won't make a difference to your empty bank account. There are millions of ways to make money on the internet but it all comes down to one thing, Action!. Without action nothing can change.

Some Easy ways to make money on the internet are article marketing and pay per visit marketing. These two techniques are used by millions online to make hundreds and thousands of dollars a month.

Article marketing is a type of advertising by writing short articles related to business' respective industry. Once written, the author makes these articles freely available for distribution and publication in the marketplace via article directories such as Ezinearticles.com.

Pay per visit (PPC) is an advertising model used on search engines, advertising networks, and content websites/blogs, where advertisers only pay when a user actually visits on an ad to visit the advertiser's website.

Why are they easy ways to make money on the internet?

Well Article marketing is the only way I believe in the world that can make you money without spending money. Actually to be more correct can make ANYONE money without spending money. Its just a simple matter of taking action.

PPC cost a bit of money but if the foundation is properly learnt and applied then making thousands of dollars a day can be easily done. However many people do not have the proper foundation and "RUSH" into PPC thinking it is very easy. This is when people lose hundreds of dollars online and quit. There are many websites out there that offer to teach you the foundation of article marketing and PPC marketing. From my experiences I would suggest Wealthy Affiliate <http://www.wealthyaffiliatesnow.info> Why? Because their information is broken down so that even a toddler can understand.

Heard Enough? Come read my success <http://www.squidoo.com/Buywealthlyaffiliatesnow> with Wealthy Affiliate!

Learn Affiliate Marketing Today - How I Finally Did It

If someone had told me a year ago that I could learn affiliate marketing today and actually make money online, I would not have believed them. Trying to make money on the internet can be an incredibly frustrating task. There are so many "opportunities" out there, whether legitimate or not, you get stuck trying to find one that will work. I have tried so many of those opportunities in the last 5 years I was beginning to wonder if any of them were actually real and worked for others or if perhaps there was something wrong with me!

I was about to give up my search for a way to make money online when out of the blue, simply by trying yet another opportunity, I ran across an incredible online school that has taught me how to become a successful internet marketer. Since I had already tried to do affiliate marketing I knew a little about it and didn't think it would work for me.

The information they provided taught me how to create a website, write articles and advertise on the internet for free without using the pay-per-visit method which is what I had tried before. There are too many layers to internet marketing for me to have learned everything I needed to know to learn affiliate marketing today without this online school. Buying a million resources or even going back to a traditional school just wasn't an option for me. I didn't have that kind of money to begin with, which is why I had been looking for money making opportunities online.

I am a stay-at-home mother of 2 and simply wanted to be able to make some extra money from home to help contribute to my family. Before I started to learn how to do internet marketing I had wasted so much money on other programs online with no success. I have been so pleased by this online school it has finally allowed me the financial freedom I've been looking for.

Wealthy Affiliate helped me to learn affiliate marketing today <http://www.squidoo.com/learn-affiliate-marketing-today> and because of their help I have seen my world change around me.

I created a website http://www.we-pay-it-forward.com sharing the resources that helped me finally succeed at internet marketing, in the hopes that anyone else looking for the same opportunity won't have to look so far. I hope you find these resources as helpful as I did!

Internet Home Jobs

Are you seeking a good job at home and through the internet? If you want a very good part time or even full time job online just read this article and you'll discover how easy it is to start a very profitable home online job in a very short time.

I want to tell you that there is a perfect home internet job that is called Affiliate Marketing. Simply, affiliate marketing could be the number one internet job from home and the best thing is anyone around the world can join this business to make living income.

To start your affiliate marketing business you need to search for a valuable product through the internet, try to find something you already know about or at least you want to know about. This is because you will encourage others to buy that product so you need to know all benefits of it.

After you find a good product, you can join its affiliate program. There are some good affiliate programs that give you up to 75% for every sell you made. After joining the affiliate program, you will be provided by a personal affiliate link that you can promote and everyone can buy the product through your affiliate link. You will get a commission.

Say that the product you've chosen has a price of $40, and the merchant gives you %75 of the price, you can preserve a nice $30 every sell you made. Say that you're making one sell per day, this means $900 per month and $10800 per year and this is only for one product. Yes, you can repeat your successful campaign for as many products as you want. The amount of money you can doing from the internet home jobs is up to you, you can easily make a good living income doing only affiliate marketing.

Learn how to make money online, step by step programs reviewed: http://www.homeonlinejobs.net/opportunities.htm

Read more with my website: http://www.homeonlinejobs.net <http://www.homeonlinejobs.net/>

Affiliate Marketing - 3 Fast Money Maker For New Affiliates

Two Tier Programs

While search engines, e-mail, and website syndication capture much of the attention of online retailers, affiliate marketing carries a much lower profile. With this program CDNOW was the first non-adult website to introduce the concept of an affiliate or associate program with its idea of visit-through purchasing.

As an Affiliate I Prefer to Use Two Tier Programs Here's 5 reasons why.

While search engines, e-mail, and website syndication capture much of the attention of online retailers, affiliate marketing carries a much lower profile. With this program CDNOW was the first non-adult website to introduce the concept of an affiliate or associate program with its idea of visit-through purchasing. The phrase, "Affiliates are an extended sales force for your business", which is often used to explain affiliate marketing, is not completely accurate. Two-tier programs exist in the minority of affiliate programs; most are simply one-tier. Two-tier programs exist in the minority of affiliate programs; most are simply one-tier. Referral programs beyond two-tier involve multi-level marketing MLM or network marketing.

While search engines, e-mail, and website syndication capture much of the attention of online retailers, affiliate marketing carries a much lower profile. With this program CDNOW was the first non-adult website to introduce the concept of an affiliate or associate program with its idea of visit-through purchasing. The phrase, "Affiliates are an extended sales force for your business", which is often used to explain affiliate marketing, is not completely accurate. Two-tier programs exist in the minority of affiliate programs; most are simply one-tier. Two-tier programs exist in the minority of affiliate programs; most are simply one-tier. Referral programs beyond two-tier involve multi-level marketing MLM or network marketing.

. Affiliate Marketing - My 3 Favorite Ways Make Money as an Affiliate

1. I love two tier programs for many reasons and would take to many words to explain it on this article but I will cut it short for you today.

This first make money idea is using a two tier affiliate program, which it has to be a niche that has a large audience. They have to really need this product such as a high blood pressure cures, Ring Tone Downloads and so on. Here's where the easy money comes in. You want to Broker these sites to similar sites and ezines. Here are a few must haves for the product site you are brokering for.

1. They must pay you at least $10 on the second tier. (I will explain why later)

2. They must provide some useful marketing tool, Banners are a must are no deal.

3. Must have at least a one year cookie. . (I will explain why later)

4. They must have a great product at a reasonable price.

The reason You need them to pay at least $10 is because you profits will easier to track, and the reason they should have a one year cookie is that if someone don't buy right away and lets say buys 2 or 3 months later you will still get credit for the sell.

Here is how you will make money brokering these site.

A. Locate on Google similar site to your niche you are bordering for and email the editor or owner of the site and

B. Explain that the product that you sell is similar to the one the website owner is marketing or has ezine about.

C. Convince them that if they simply place a banner or text ad on their site from the product you are selling. They will make easy money by displaying the banner or sending out emails to their existing list, which could be very large.

It will be a great feeling when you wake up a look on your affiliate site and see loads of sells going into your account without spending any money to get it.

2. Gifting Type Programs

Have you even heard about these programs because you usually have to be invited into it and some are a little different in structure? In a gifting type program you would have to a one up or two up and some even three up structure, what this means is that lets say it cost you $100 dollars to join with the good ones you will be offered a site of your own to market the program. Most of these programs you will get loads of usable software and ebook by the hundreds some times, that you can give away as gifts to your visitors or sell with complete resale rights. Getting back to the program, you now have to bring in another person though advertising and once you get one you would have to give that first person and their $100 to the person that brought you in. If it is a 2up program you would have to give the first 2 people and their $200 to the person whom brought you in. Now you would be qualified to receive gifts of $100. Now when you bring in the next person in they will have to give you their $100 and their next two people $100.

So with 2 people they both would gave you when their next two new people you will make $200 and that keep on forever. I really make good money from these program but you have to know how to market them right. But they can make a Hugh amount of money fast. I would love to tell you how much I make doing this but I don't think you would believe me. Are they legal? Yes because you are also buying products. There are different types of these program and can be very expensive to participate in, the one I started out which was not a good experience, I paid $500 to participate but without knowing how to market the program I just stop advertising to soon and forgot it for a while that is until I had received some online marketing training.

3. Selling Advertisement a an Affiliate

Selling advertising can be a great way to make money online because everyone with a website that sales anything will need to advertise.

You Must advertise if you want traffic to come to your site. Therefore, If you are selling online advertising you won't have to worry about is ever going out of style or there never be a time when it won't be needed.

So, selling advertisement as an affiliate can be a none stop, recession proof, way to make money online. There are many good advertising agency out there such a rent-a-list which offers targeted emails, Text Ads, solo email, lottery email, and much more. They offer great affiliate tools and that's a must for me. For me to promote their product they must have at the very least banners.

I like to setup a squeeze page of my own to sent my customers and that usually offer them free ebooks to capture the customer's information.

If you don't know what a squeeze page is just go to Google and type squeeze page generator and you will get lots of examples.

So, If you sell the advertising niche you stand a good chance of make money that last for years and years.

Tommy Lee, has been an online affiliate for 4 years and commits himself to help new people to the make money online sector of business with their marketing needs and training needs.

If this information was of any help to you and you feel you need more marketing training please check out this website with free video training for anyone looking to lean how to advertise online in a way that will make you real and steady income. Visit http://www.tarbuckle.ws

5 Ways to Get That First Affiliate Marketing Check

There are Kommandos, Black Hats, Big Dogs, Guerillas, Boot Camps, Underground strategies, Assassins and people who want to sell you something that will annihilate the opposition, kill the competition.

For newbies to Internet Marketing it looks like you're getting ready to be shipped out to Afghanistan or Iraq rather than sitting down at your computer and making a couple of thousands pounds/dollars/euros or whatever a month.

The big hitters fail to realize that for the majority of people, that amount is a fortune, they seem to think we all want to be multi-millionaires and have unlimited cash to make that dream come true. When really most of the people who try affiliate marketing or even eBay are doing so, because it's a less expensive way to kick off their new business.

But have you noticed that once you link up with a product, your inbox receives an avalanche of "you can't miss out on this" offers, because if you do you all your competitors are going to stuff your attempts at making any cash.

Look at the testimonials of these offers and you'll see the same guys time and again extolling the virtues of these must have products.

For the newbie this is the start of information overload.

They're so busy trying to read all the bonuses to make any money. I recently saw one that had 75 hours of training videos. 75 hours!!!!

Life's just too short, it looks great as a free bonus but tell me who's going to sit for 75 hours and watch those.

So here's my advice for newbies if they want to get that first affiliate check from Visitbank or where ever. And by the way when the first check appears, you will be hooked!

1 Don't get hung up over the technology.

In affiliate marketing, you don't need to know how to build a website, write a sales letter or even organize the taking of cash or posting out the product.

For instance on Visitbank there are thousands of products offering you up to 75 per commission, they all come complete with a sales page, the product is downloaded by the customer and every fortnight a check is sent out.

A word of warning though, if you live outside the US prepare to pay hefty bank charges because for some reason Visitbank still pay in US Dollars so if you get a $100 check and want to pay it into say a UK bank, you'll pay up to £10 in charges.

When is Visitbank going to pay affiliates in their own currency through say Paypal?

2 To begin with decide what you want to earn from your online business.

And make it achievable! No point going for $30k a month that simply isn't going to happen.
Lets say its a $1000 and you like the look of a product that will give you $25 commission on each sale.

Now a $1000 seems a huge amount to raise over 30 days.

But the secret affiliate weapon for success is to break that total down.

So we know we have to make 40 sales at $25 to make our $1000..so we need to sell at least one product a day.

Breaking goals down to realistic chunks makes them so much more achievable.

3. Focus on marketing that one product until you are achieving your goal of $1000..then add another product but look for a higher commission.

Marketing. Ah well that's another area we could talk about until the cows come home.

There are various ways of doing it from buying traffic to the product website, Pay Per Visit and Google AdWords. You can try using US FreeAds, writing articles, or blogs even YouTube.

4 The next secret affiliate weapon in your armory is to be consistent in whatever area you chose.

Forget about sitting down in front of your favorite soap, get online and write that article, prepare that ad or email. So something didn't work learn from it, move on and try again.

But do something, if you don''t take action what's going to be the result?

Forget about getting rich overnight, concentrate on doing something, not matter how small, everyday to push the business forward.

5 If you're focused, and consistent it's because you've picked out the other secret affiliate weapon and that's commitment.

You don't just need a goal of say $1000 a month, you want to focus on the real reason behind that goal.

Visualize it, touch it, it smell it.

It maybe the payment on a dream car, one installment on a once-in-a-life time round the world trip or even something as simple as allowing you more time with family and friends or to pursue your favorite hobby, buy the latest camera or fishing rod.

Whatever it is, being committed is a major factor in bringing you nearer your goal.

I know I had a go at the military sounding names used by many of the big hitters but I believe if you use the secret affiliate weapons of focus, consistency and commitment then you'll be successful.

Remember there are millions of people who dream of being financially successful. But there are only a chosen few who wake up and make it happen.

Which one are you?

I'm a UK based radio journalist with a wife, three cats and two mortgages to support.

If my article has whet your appetite and you want to dip your toes into the murky but lucrative waters of affiliate marketing then check out my site.

http://www.infoproductslibrary.com

Money Through Affiliate Marketing - The Truth About Making it Work For You

The advertising industry that exists on the web is a fascinating yet complex entity. A lot of people do earn very good money through affiliate marketing. Most people who start up in the affiliate advertising field don't realize there is a right way and a wrong way to go about the task. This is the reason that most newcomers to the industry fail.

You can't cheat the system and win when you are trying to create a financial future. The problem is that people don't realize that they will only get out of affiliate marketing what they put into it. In order to make money with affiliate programs you have to work hard at it. You can't just buy a website and slap a bunch of banners on it and call yourself a marketer. So many people want the easy way out and that is what is wrong with their incomes. Or perhaps I should say their lack of income.

You are going to spend a lot of time doing research and finding out where the money is. You also better know something about what you are trying to market. If you want to make affiliate commissions on something you know zip about, you can. But first you will have to immerse yourself in that subject and learn it inside and out. Or you could hire a specialist to do that part of the work for you. This gets really expensive though and could cost you most of your money through affiliate marketing income.

You won't make windfall cash overnight as an affiliate marketer. It takes time to get everything researched and put together. Then you must patiently wait until the search engines fully index your pages so people find you online. You must also spend a lot of time spreading links to carry inbound traffic to you. It does pay off well if you stick to your guns.

If you want to discover a quick and effective way to make money online <http://theonlinemoneysecret.com/> all you have to do is Go here <http://theonlinemoneysecret.com/> .

How to Turn Your Hobby Into a Paycheque

Online affiliate training abounds, and there are dozens of forums and websites waiting to offer advice and knowledge to people wishing to make money online. But do you have what it takes to be a successful affiliate marketer?

Everyone has interests and hobbies. From reading books to listening to music, watching movies, playing sports, writing stories or traveling, we all have things we enjoy doing. But are you making money at sharing your expertise and enthusiasm, and if you are not, the question is "why not"? Thousands of people are turning their hobby expertise into profits, by promoting affiliate products online that fit into their sphere of knowledge. It is fun, creative, exciting and extremely lucrative. So, what does it take to turn your passion into profit?

Making money by promoting something we love is everyone's dream, especially if we can do it from home with very little - to no- overhead. Affiliate marketing is a revenue sharing partnership between a web merchant and one or more affiliates (online marketers), where the affiliate is paid a commission for sending visits, leads or sales to the merchant. There are many ways to do this, and the advantage is that you don't need a product idea, or have the upfront costs of creating your own product. You also don't have to worry about e-commerce or bookkeeping, or even customer support! It is awesome! That is why many so many people are going online now to supplement their income or replace their jobs. Affiliate marketing is a great way to earn money, and although there is a global recession, online purchasing continues to grow. The market is huge and the demand for affiliates is wide open.

However, becoming learned and successful at affiliate marketing is not as easy as many people think when they first get started. It is important to get the proper kind of online affiliate training, or you will very quickly get confused and overwhelmed. Online affiliate training is in abundance online, however, reading eBooks, forums, or taking tutorials is not the best way to learn this industry. These cover only a miniscule area of this vast topic and would be like trying to learn how to run before you learn how to walk.

So before you begin your venture into affiliate marketing, you need to decide first how you will learn the industry and effective marketing strategies. There is an online Affiliate Marketing University called Wealthy Affiliate University which teaches you using an 8 week action plan, videos, certified training courses, eBooks, tutorials, and forums. It is regarded by many to be the best affiliate training available on the Internet, and well worth considering. You will soon discover that in order to become a good affiliate marketer you must possess perseverance, patience and determination. Too many affiliates fail because they become impatient, which is where an action plan becomes instrumental.

To be an affiliate marketer is not an easy task. There is a lot to learn and finding the right online affiliate training is the first step in turning your hobby into an extremely lucrative career.

Get $1000 worth of FREE business eBooks and software at http://www.wealthy-affiliate-university-bonus.info

4 Key Strategies to Making Money Online With Affiliate Marketing With Little Or No Money

As long as you have access to a computer and an internet connection, you will be able to earn money.

Blogging

One of the most popular affiliate marketing business models these days is blogging. You can get started blogging for free using a hosted blog solution like Blogger.com. I don't recommend this if you have the money to invest for a domain and web hosting, but it's a good way to get started if you don't. Blogging requires you to be at least moderately skilled in writing. You need to be consistent, because you need to be capable of posting to your blog on a regular basis, at least once per week. One of the big secrets to success with blogging is to update often. Google loves fresh content, and they like to rank it high in their results. Posting regularly helps keep your blog fresh, and it will eventually help it rank well. If you don't like to write, or if you don't feel you could be consistent enough to update regularly, blogging might not be the right business model for you.

Bum Marketing

Web 2.0, Bum Marketing, Article Marketing - Web 2.0 marketing, also called bum marketing, uses completely free methods of making money. This is why it's called "bum marketing"... because it's done without money. Basically, you write articles and submit them to various places that accept free articles. Then you can include your affiliate advertisements on those sites. There are many different sites you can use this way. EzineArticles.com is perhaps the most popular. It is an article directory, and users can write articles and add them to the directory in order to have a couple of links in a box at the end of the article. This box, known as the "resource box", "bio box", or "author box", can house affiliate links (although you must link to a domain that is being forwarded to the affiliate link) or a link to a site you own. This site can be another web 2.0 site like Squidoo.com or Blogger.com. You can also use the articles you write to make web pages on sites like Squidoo.com, HubPages.com, and Weebly.com. These sites are free to use, and you can use them to promote your affiliate offerings.

Review Sites

Review sites have been taking the internet by storm recently. They are a super way to make money with affiliate products, because so many people like to search for reviews of products before they buy them. You will ideally want your own domain for this to give it more credibility. You might buy something like www.CoffeePotReviews.com if you wanted to review various coffee pot models. In order to appear completely impartial, you would want to give some models a poor review, others average, and only a few models a really good review. Also, you'd want to be sure that you didn't give the most expensive items the best reviews. That would look very fishy to your visitors. The only way review sites work is if the visitor truly believes the reviews are impartial and unbiased.

Pay-Per-Visit Marketing

PPC marketing is a fantastic way to make money with affiliate products, but it does take a lot of thought, planning, and practice. It is very common to lose money for a while in PPC, until you learn how to set up profitable campaigns. PPC takes quite a bit of investment. Although most PPC companies don't require you to pay up front, you will have to pay your bill in about a month. If you don't pay, your ads could be suspended, and you could even lose your account and be banned for life. The problem is, most affiliate marketing companies won't pay you in time for you to pay for your PPC marketing costs. A lot of affiliate companies pay monthly, or even quarterly. The checks might not arrive before your bill is due. Plus, if you spend a lot of money, sometimes the company will require you to pay for your visits ahead of time. For example, if you suddenly ran up $500 in visits at Google AdWords, they might temporarily halt your ads until you paid for the $500 you had already spent. Considering that you could easily spend $500 in a single day if you set up a lot of campaigns with large daily limits, you might lose your account way before your affiliate check ever arrives.

If you would like to find out More and Earn $27,379-$43,768 EVERY week. PLUS be Directly Taught By An Online Millionaire and start earning money TODAY then simply go to>>

http://www.Make-Money-At-HomeNow.com

To Read a Comprehensive review of this amazing Money Making System...

http://www.Make-Money-At-HomeNow.com

7 Key Steps to Affiliate Marketing Success

Bum Marketing

Bum Marketing Bum marketing makes use of many free online resources for generating traffic. You can promote affiliate products directly with bum marketing, or you can send traffic to another website or blog. There are different types of bum marketing. Article marketing is the most well-known type, and involves submitting articles to online repositories known as article directories. You can promote affiliate products directly with article marketing, but some of the article directories require you to use a domain name to forward to the affiliate link. Using sites like Squidoo.com and HubPages.com also allows you to get traffic from search engines based on their high PageRank and authority.

SEO

SEO or search engine optimization, is perhaps the most important way to get high-quality traffic. SEO traffic is usually very good, because people who are searching for something are often ready to buy. Let's say you create a review site that reviews several popular digital camera models. Would you rather have a visitor who visits a link from another website out of curiosity, or would you rather have a visitor who has searched for "buy X model digital camera"? The person who has searched for "buy X model digital camera" is almost definitely ready to buy, or at least researching a potential purchase. But someone who visited a link to your site from another site might not be very interested in digital cameras at all! They may have visited the link simply because they were bored, or curious.

The title serves two purposes for SEO:

1. It is very important to search rankings, because search engines assume that the title expresses the main point of a page.

2. It is what attracts visitors to visit the link to visit your site when they see it in the SERPs.

Your title needs to contain at least one main keyword phrase, as well as be interesting enough to visit. Your most important keyword phrase should be the first, because prominence is important. Search engines assume that the keywords that appear earlier are more important. You need to have a different title for every page on your site, and that title should relate to the topic of the page.

Blog Commenting

Blog commenting is a very good way to get traffic. It can be beneficial for two purposes. First, it can bring visitors directly from the links when they read your comment. And second, it gives you relevant backlinks to your site to help improve your search engine rankings. The trouble is, many of your blog comments are NOT going to help your SEO.

Social Marketing

Social networking sites like Facebook, and microblogging sites like Twitter offer you a world of new marketing opportunities. They have hundreds of thousands, sometimes millions of users that you can get in touch with. But using social marketing is a delicate process. You have to know the rules of the various sites very well, and you have to be prepared to follow them to the letter.

Forum Marketing

Forum marketing is, in many ways, more delicate than social marketing. Forums are usually owned by individuals or small companies rather than large corporations, like most social networking sites. Because of this smaller atmosphere, it is much easier to be noticed, singled out, and banned. You have to be a lot more careful, because every post you make has the potential to be seen by every single member of a forum, not just the individuals on a list of friends or the people you privately send messages to.

Viral Marketing

Viral marketing, simply put, is the process of bringing in traffic by producing marketing material that will spread from user to user. Viral marketing is usually very funny, exciting, bizarre, or in some way something to be talked about. In order for something to go viral, it needs to be something that is actually so interesting that people will naturally want to talk about it. If people see it, and are interested, the will watch it and remember it. But it has to be something really special for people to talk about it and for it to spread. Viral marketing is a great way to bring in traffic. It's also one of the most difficult to get right. It can be very difficult to anticipate what will go viral.

It's best if you get someone who is experienced in creating viral marketing campaigns to help you. Just make sure to ask for references and proof of past success before you agree to pay them

Guest Authoring

Guest authoring is a bit like article marketing, but you write for popular blogs or websites instead of submitting to article directories. This benefits the owner of the blog or site, because they get free content, and it benefits you because you get the publicity and a relevant backlink.

Who Do You Believe?

When you set up your own business online it is essential that you keep track of information that is relevant to your and your niche.

The problem is that you can be sent or read information that either isn't 100% accurate or is heavily tainted by the writers point of view. This is especially true if you get any level of your information from forums.

When you start off in affiliate marketing you will most likely go to at least one or two forums looking for advice and help and there is usually some great information that will help you manage your business. However in amongst all the good solid business advice that will help you build your income and your business there will also be negative posts.

I can almost guarantee that no matter what service you are using for payment or which affiliate management program you go with there will be someone with a negative view of it. I know that sounds harsh but it is true.

In my early days I spent far to much time listening to the negative people and not enough time building my business. It is a tough balancing act but you need to balance the facts (if there are any) with the risks involved.

Affiliate marketing is no different to an offline business, you will have people not pay you, you will have products or marketing pushes that you thought would be profitable turn out to be duds, you will lose money on some things. I can also guarantee that every one of those things will annoy you and make you stronger.

Affiliate marketing is a business and you are in charge of how big your business becomes!

I love affiliate marketing, but I hate messing about with Wordpress code so I had the Affiliate marketing plugin <http://www.wpeasyads.com/> made to manage my ads on my Wordpress sites. http://www.wpeasyads.com/ is the simplest way to increase your affiliate income.

3 Tips to Help Every Affiliate Survive

Every affiliate marketer is always on the lookout for the successful market that gives the largest return on an investment. Really, it is more complicated than that. It is just good selling practices that were proved over years of tough work and dedication.

What are these 3 tactics?

1. Using unique net pages to plug each separate product you are marketing. Don't pile the whole thing together solely to save some cash on Internet hosting.

Always include product reviews on the internet site so visitors will have a preliminary understanding on what the product can do to those that buy them. Be certain that these buyers are way more than ready to permit you to use their names and testimonials on the site of the precise product you're selling.

You can also write articles highlighting the uses of the product and include them on the internet site as a further page. Make the pages tasty and forceful and include calls to action in the info.

2. Offer free reports to your readers. According to those in the know, a sale is closed customarily on the 7th contact with a prospect.

Only 2 things can potentially happen with the web page alone : closed sale or the prospect leaving the page and never return again. By placing helpful info into their inboxes at certain mentioned times, you may remind them of the product they desire ,before they find out the sale is closed.

Don't make it sound like a sales spiel.

Include compelling subject lines in the e-mail. Convince those that signed up to your free reports that they are going to be missing something giant if they don't take action on your services and products.

3. Get the sort of traffic that is focused to your product.

Just think, if the person who visited your internet site has no interest whatsoever in what you are offering, they're going to be among those who move on and never come back. Write articles for publication in e-zines and e-reports. This way you can find publications that are targeting your target market and what you have put up might just grab their interest.

Jack is a 66yr old retired business owner, who was forced into retirement early when he was the victim of a violent crime. Jack found the online world so he could work from home.Its been a long strange trip for Jack, but after allot of time and attending the school of hard Knox, he has become successful,you can visit Jack at http://www.jackggordon.com

Make Money on Internet in Just a Few Visits With Visitbank!

You have probably been hearing and reading about the Internet being a goldmine of money for savvy entrepreneurs with little more than a computer and an Internet connection. Well, it is true!

In fact, you can make money on Internet in just a few visits of the mouse with Visitbank. Here is how it works. (This is very important because ignorance of the working of the Internet can cost you dearly in lost revenues)

True to its name, Visitbank allows individuals to earn passive income through affiliate marketing ? customers visit on the products advertised on your website, they pay a visit and pay for products on the advertisers? sites, and you get paid for your referrals. It?s quite simple, really.

CB is one of the biggest, if not the biggest, retailer over the Internet of software products and digital information. Thus, you are assured of the authenticity of the products featured therein.

And speaking of products, there are 10,000 advertisers of web-based products at Visitbank. This means that you can make money on Internet on at least 10,000 products, with the assumption that each advertiser only has one product (not very likely) and that you can feature all 10,000 products (again, not very likely).

However, you can maximize your income on Visitbank without featuring all 10,000 advertisers. Besides, it?s not a wise idea to feature just about every product that takes your fancy and every product that is pushed at you simply because 10,000 ads on your website will drive away traffic.

Thus, it is important to choose products that answer the needs and wants of your target audience. This way, you will become relevant to them, not to mention, be able to tie up your website?s contents with the products advertised.

For example, don?t feature an ad about adorable pets when your website deals with animal allergy. It?s common sense, really.

Of course, other considerations come into play. To make money on Internet via the Visitbank products, you can choose according to the products? popularity and the percentage of commissions paid (as much as 75% on some products although you should aim for not less than 25%).

Let?s assume that you have a website and you want to become a member, of which the first concern would be the payment of membership fees. Fortunately for cash-strapped entrepreneurs, Visitbank allows you to make money on Internet without breaking the bank precisely because it is free.

Just make an account and start promoting your products. It?s passive income precisely because you can just wait for your commissions to come even when you do nothing beyond your first few promotional efforts.

You will get paid 15 days after the end of each period, which ends on the first and sixteenth day of each month. So, basically, you have a monthly income that can even beat the income of your regular 9-to-5 job with the obnoxious supervisor.

Indeed, when you want to make money on Internet, why sweat it out when you can milk Visitbank for all its worth? Who knows? Someday, you might even be able to sell your own methodologies and systems to others, thereby, earning more money for you while helping others.

Eric Stein is a marketer for a website that explains how to make money on the internet <http://make-money-visitbank.com> . He has been getting paid by Visitbank for over 10 years now, checkout his website: http://make-money-visitbank.com

Affiliate Commission - Dumping the Beliefs That Are Holding You Back

Earning an affiliate commission is all about follow through. If you are using a good system, the only thing standing in your way is, well, you. I know that sounds funny, but if you aren't currently living the life you you'd like to be, then you have somehow been able to stop yourself from successfully doing the things that you know you should do. One way people do this is with faulty beliefs.

Without beliefs we would struggle to do everything. Because you have a belief that chairs will hold you when you sit down, you don't have to cautiously test each one before you have a seat. The generalization, or belief about this class of objects we call "chairs" allows you to just take a seat, and use the mental space that has been freed up by your belief, to be used for something else. Without our beliefs, each day would be like the first day with everything- we'd get nothing done.

Now, some of the beliefs we have are no longer accurate, and need updated, or worse yet, they were never accurate. At one time we believed that we caught a cold if we didn't have a hat on when it was cold outside. Later, scientists told us that a cold is caused by a virus and that whether we had a hat on, or not, really didn't matter. But I'll bet if you stop and think about it, you still know someone who tells their kids "Get your hat on before you go outside or you'll catch a cold!"

One way I've found to quickly "pull the plug" on beliefs that are no longer serving me well, is to find counter-examples to the belief I'd like to ditch once and for all. If, for example, I've had a belief that say's "I can't be the head of that organization, I'm too young!" I'll immediately research and find at least 10 examples of people my age that were in fact, the head of a particular organization or group.

Once you have irrefutable evidence to the contrary, it becomes almost impossible to hang on to your old way of processing the world.

So, what beliefs about your abilities as an affiliate marketer have you allowed to block your progress? Hunt them down, write them down, and then, spotlight them with hard evidence that represents the other end of the possibility spectrum. Working through the beliefs that have been like dead weight, and then inserting a new, empowering belief in its place will put you on the path to online success.

Vincent Harris is a Body Language Expert and the author of The Productivity Epiphany. Vince long ago realized the value of passive income offered by affiliate marketing. His personal website is http://www.VinceHarris.com and you can find out what his latest discovery is in the world on affiliate income at http://www.PeaceOfMindMoney.com

Affiliate Marketing Programs - The Gift of the Recession

Affiliate marketing programs offer the average person the opportunity to experience life on their own terms. Once you have replaced your former "job" income, you can enjoy making your own schedule, taking a day off when you want, and not having to ask or "beg", and a whole host of other worthy advantages. What you may not realize, however, is that the current recession has provided those doing affiliate marketing an opportunity like never before.

Right now, people are looking for answers with more tenacity, fervor and fear than at any other time in recent history. It doesn't matter what they are looking for. They might be searching for a home remedy to remove warts, or an internet marketing online business to be able to retire early. It doesn't matter. Chances are, there is an affiliate marketing program that will address their concern and provide them with the answer they are looking for.

Are you seizing this opportunity? See, when things are good, and the economy is booming, people may have more money to spend online, but when they are nervous, stressed out and fearful, not only will they find the money they need to purchase the ebook that will provide them with relief, they'll buy more digital products in this situation than in any other.

Just look at what happened after 9/11. There had been companies that sold gas masks for decades. But all it took was one attack, and millions of people suddenly realized they had a problem that they didn't have the day before; they didn't own a gas mask in case of a chemical attack. In a quest to search for and find a solution, many of the companies that carried the gas masks sold out in days.

As an affiliate marketer, that's what you do; you provide people with the solutions they are seeking, and you get paid for doing so. The more people you help, the more money you make. It's really just as simple as that.

Take advantage of the current opportunity, and the gift that has been handed to affiliate marketers by the economic recession.

Vincent Harris is a Body Language Expert and the author of The Productivity Epiphany. Vince realizes the advantage of a passive income stream through affiliate marketing. His personal website is http://www.VinceHarris.com and his latest discovery in affiliate marketing can be found at http://www.PeaceOfMindMoney.com

Affiliate Internet Marketing - The Importance of a Well Formed Goal

Affiliate internet marketing offers virtually anyone the opportunity to live a life that those who are not in the "know" can't even imagine. You let others create outstanding and beneficial products, and then, you simply help them make those who would benefit from their digital product aware that it exists. Can it get any easier than that? There is one thing, however, that can stand between your affiliate internet marketing successes.

As you probably know, having a goal is important. In fact, I'm sure you've heard about goals so much, by now, that you are starting to feel like you could get by without hearing any more about them. By the way, I felt like that too. Like most people who succeed, though, I finally figured out that not having a goal was a good way to kiss what I wanted "bye-bye!"

A goal is not a goal though; not all goals are created equal. Goals that actually cause us to fail, look like any other goal-at first glance. Closer examination, however, reveals a significant and potentially devastating difference.

The kind of goal that will "doom" your success is one that you don't control. Meaning, if I say "I'm going to sell 50 boxes of cookies today" I have established an outcome that requires people that I can influence, but NOT control, to buy 50 boxes of cookies. What I DO control, is how many people I talk to; what methods I use to persuade them, etc. Those are things I DO control, and therefore, I have a goal that will not promote self-sabotage.

There are several factors to a well formed goal, and I'll outline them now.

1. Make sure your goal is stated in terms of what you DO want, not what you don't want. When I am working with a client, I always begin by asking them what they want. Many will reply by telling me what they DON'T want. They'll say, "Well, I don't want to be so unorganized and messy anymore."

The problem with this answer is that it only presents their mind with images of what they no longer want, but it does not provide a crystal clear image of what they'd like instead. If you know what you don't want, you're half way home. Just determine what you WOULD rather have, do, be or experience.

2. Be clear about when and where you want this result. If someone wants to be energetic and hard charging, that might be a great goal at work, but can you see where this might cause a problem in a relationship? Nothing is "good" or "bad"; things are either useful or not, and that depends on the context. Being overly assertive may work well for an attorney in the courtroom. But if he carries this same behavior into his relationship with his children, it may cause problems.

3. Is it something you can achieve by yourself? If not, be clear about whose help you might need. Remember, if your goal involves too many variables that you cannot control, you'll proba-

bly get frustrated and quit. Build your goals around the things you do control; the actions that will lead to your desired outcome.

4. Have a clear understanding of the wider scope of influence that achieving your goal will have. Some goals, while very exciting to you, may require so much on your part that they do not make a positive contribution to the people you care about. If this is the case, and you don't know it, you'll likely engage in self-sabotage at some point, to restore the needed order to your life.

There you have it. When you can align your affiliate internet marketing goals with the four points listed above, you'll find yourself moving forward, and your bank balance going up in record time.

Vincent Harris is a Body Language Expert and the author of The Productivity Epiphany. Vince realizes the value of passive income created through affiliate marketing. His website is http://www.VinceHarris.com, and his latest discovery for increasing your internet affiliate income can be found at http://www.PeaceOfMindMoney.com

Tips on Affiliate Referrals

So you've got yourself signed up for a new two-tier affiliate program and are excited to start promoting the program to increase your earnings. You've done some work to promote the program you are referring people to but are ready to try some more tactics. Here are some more ideas you should consider when trying to generate affiliate referrals:

Dig deeper and they will follow.

The folks you are trying to sell on the affiliate plan aren't dumb or naïve, they're serious internet marketers (at least we hope they are, you're banking on them being able to sell!). Take the time, make the commitment - do your research, write an in-depth post with more information than a reader is liable to get anywhere else, and you will get more incoming traffic, better search engine rankings for your keywords, and, this is the goal, more referrals. Why should your readers try the program you're referring them to if they don't think you know what you're doing? They don't want to waste their time after all. So get serious---the best way to build the trust you need to generate referrals is to be obviously masterful in your knowledge.

Trackbacks are not backtracking . . . they're the way forwards.

When you reference other people's work on your subject it does a few things. For one, a trackback will generate a link to your post beneath the original work you are referencing. This is very handy because someone reading the original article may be searching for more information about it and since you're providing more information . . . you get the idea. Secondly, by referencing others' work you're showing that you're not a plagiarist (ie you're an honest dealer) and also lets people see what kind of original ideas you have. If these are good, you'll build trust and confidence and . . . you guessed it, referrals.

Build links in your community.

A service like Google Alerts can let you set up a notification whenever a blogger writes a post on the topic you're interested in. When you get an alert, you can read the post and post a relevant comment along with a link to your post. But don't spam by simply promoting yourself, contribute the discussion of the original post. You should, after all, have something to contribute here after your own research and writing. Include pertinent, useful information in your comment and then reference your link for people to access more information if they're interested. This is both polite and good for business--- no one's going to visit on your context-less link unless you let them know why they should.

About the Author: Peter Ryan is an online marketer and representative of Adapp Solutions, Inc., providing affiliate networks <http://www.hasoffers.com> and advertisers with powerful web-based technology.

Affiliate Marketing Online Program - Making Money From Home Could Not Be Easier

More and more people these days turn to an affiliate marketing online program to earn a full time income from home. In today's volatile economy and unexpected job losses, saddened and downtrodden people have to apply for new jobs elsewhere for income opportunities. Now, if these same people, who worked in the real workforce, have any knowledge of the Internet, they can begin making money today with affiliate marketing. Sad to say though, many people are not aware that this type of opportunity exists and the amount of money one can make from it.

Affiliate Marketing in a Nutshell

Many might wonder what affiliate marketing is. Affiliate marketing, in a nutshell, is promoting products from an already established online, or offline, company. The affiliate marketer, probably you, can then get a percentage or commission, of however many products are purchased from your blog or website. Because working with an affiliate marketing online program is an easy way to earn an income from home, more and more people, especially stay at home mom's, are able to stay home and make money. Now, depending on what 'niche' an individual finds themselves in, they can look online for just about any program or product to promote which fancies them.

Beginners to Affiliate Marketing

If anyone is looking for a way to earn money with a little effort, affiliate marketing is where they need to turn. Remember above, I talked about a website or blog? Well, having one of these would be something great to have or create. Websites, for the most part, take more time to update and reconfigure, whereas a blog page can be created, updated and written on any given day, personally, by the blog creator. So usually, blogs are the easiest way to begin.

So, when it comes to making an income from home with an affiliate marketing online program, it is wise to first create a personal, or business, blog page. If you are looking for a free blog hosting website, Blogger.com is the best place to register with and begin your journey into creative writing, business writing or both.

Use the Product Yourself

Now, it is best to be an affiliate's customer too, that way you personally know the product you are promoting. Then you can give an honest review of the product and people will trust you enough to buy from you. Even if you purchase one product, at least you have tried it and can write intelligently about it. As an affiliate marketer, you are the one sharing your experiences with said affiliate marketing online program and when you write positively about this program, they and you win.

Find out how to earn $100 per day online within 30 days with an affiliate marketing online program <http://www.squidoo.com/100-per-day-entrepreneur-profit> along with 20 other methods to make money online.

Affiliate Marketing - The Psychology of Wealth

When it comes to affiliate marketing, there are countless digital products out there to choose from. While most people are initially drawn to the idea of making money online by their desire to have a certain kind of lifestyle, unless they truly understand the psychology of wealth, they'll find it hard to do anything but barely make a living.

The mainstay of making money is paradoxical; in order to make a great deal of money, you have to shift your focus entirely away from money. Does this sound confusing and at odds with what you've read just about everywhere else? Admittedly, it is very contrarian, and yet, when you closely look at anyone who has truly become wealthy, and then maintained that wealth, you'll find that money was not the driving force. It was something far more powerful than that: contribution.

First and foremost, as an affiliate marketer, you must pick a product that rings true and resonates with something deep inside; something you know in your heart will benefit the lives of those it touches. It doesn't matter whether other affiliate marketers feel that way about this product, it is imperative, however, that YOU do.

In my own life, there was one particular ebook that focused on working through a divorce, and how to deal with the frustrations that a child custody case would introduce. This book was a true gift in my life, and as a result, I felt compelled to market this ebook and share it with others who were enduring the rigors of divorce and the like. The passion I felt about this product kept me up late at night writing articles and posting in forums and such. I never once had to "try" and get myself to do the things I needed to do to be a successful affiliate marketer. In fact, many nights I would only stop writing only because I was drifting off to sleep as I sat at my keyboard.

Interestingly enough, as time went by, and the checks started rolling in, I had almost forgotten about the fact that I was also getting paid for my efforts. See, it really didn't matter. I was focused so much on delivering the value of this product to others, that the income had become an afterthought. I never once had an income goal, or thought about how big I would like my check to be the next pay period. I was just busy doing what you do when you are compelled to add value to the lives of others.

Pick something that stirs you, something that keeps you stimulated all day and sorry that you have to go to bed. When you have aligned yourself with the products that impact you in this way, you will finally understand the psychology of wealth as it pertains to affiliate marketing.

Vincent Harris is a Body Language Expert and the author of The Productivity Epiphany. Vince long ago realized the wisdom of creating passive income streams with affiliate marketing. His personal website is http://www.VinceHarris.com and you can find his latest discovery for affiliate marketing at http://www.PeaceOfMindMoney.com

How Can I Earn Money? Affiliate Marketing Programs

Almost everyone experiences a point in their life when they ask themselves "How can I earn money?" Now, perhaps more than at any other time in recent history, literal mobs of people are asking this question. One answer is: Affiliate Marketing Programs.

Imagine, for a moment, that a good friend of yours writes a book that turns out to be hit, and he becomes a bestselling author, earning untold fortunes from this one book. You scratch your head in disbelief "I sure wish I'd have written that book!" you declare. Chances are good, that in this case, it's not that you really wish you'd have sat at your computer for countless hours, churning out page after page until the book was done. No. What you really desire is the income that the bestselling book is now earning. That's all you really want; but that seems like pure fantasy.

Affiliate marketing offers you the incredible opportunity to make that fantasy a reality. Henry David Thoreau wrote "It's not enough to be busy. The question is: What are we busy about?" Here's another question: What are YOU busy about? Thousands of other people have already written the books and recorded the mp3 audio programs that are selling like hotcakes, why shouldn't you get your fair share-and more- for simply making others aware of these often times life changing digital products?

The internet is here to stay. Once described as a "fad" the statistics tell us that every month of every year, more and more people are turning to the internet for their information, with a massive amount of that information coming in the form of digital products. If you desire to create and market your own product, that's great; you should! However, having created several programs that are currently being marketed myself, I can tell you right now, it's a whole lot easier to ride the coattails of someone else's kick butt product, and let them pay you very well for doing so.

Many of the most popular and bestselling products at Visitbank pay the affiliates that market those programs as much as 75% on each program sold. Imagine that. They have a digital product that sells for $100, and they'll pay you $75 on each sale made through your link! Countless products earn the affiliate a quick $40 per sale.

Do you realize that if you simply sold one ebook per day, 7 days a week, with a commission of $40, that you would be making $1200 per month? Bump that up to 3 ebooks per day, and you have suddenly ratcheted your monthly income to $3600, or $43,200 per year. Is this possible? Yes, I know for a fact that it is.

But isn't it true, that even $500 extra dollars per month would make a measurable difference in your life? Most people say "Yes!"

Before you run out and start waiting tables to make the few extra bucks you need each month to supplement your income, investigate the very real potential of affiliate marketing first. With the proper knowledge, and enough desire to make it happen, you could easily replace your current income in the next 12-24 months, and then start doing things on your terms. That, I might add, is a worthy goal to have.

Vincent Harris is the author of The Productivity Epiphany. Vince long ago realized the wisdom of having a passive income through affiliate marketing. http://www.PeaceOfMindMoney.com

How to Make Money on the Internet - Visitbank Products

Generalizations can cause people to needlessly stay poor. Many think "How can I make money on the internet?" but then conclude that it's just not possible for them, all because of a dangerous belief that says "If it looks too good to be true, then it probably is."

Almost anyone that has ever started to investigate the possibilities of internet affiliate marketing has uncovered the potential treasure chest of multiple income streams with Visitbank products.

Visitbank offers you the choice of an almost endless number of digital products that you can freely market as an affiliate. By searching for a product that is not only doing well, but that you also have an interest in yourself, you can profit on the mind boggling work of those who actually created the product, by simply telling others. It's really just as simple as that.

Why then, do those who are fed up with their 9-5 clock punching job, back pedal, and not go ahead and launch their own affiliate business? That too, comes down to a very simple concept. They allow a belief, a generalization about what is possible, to dictate what they will do, rather than noticing the unlimited amount of evidence in the world that proves otherwise.

You don't have to look too far at all, to find someone who is not as good looking as you are, not nearly as intelligent as you are, and frankly, who from the outside, appears to be a moron, but unlike so many others who are grumbling about how much they hate their jobs each day, they are working on their own terms, making their own schedule, and making three times as much money as everyone else. Let examples like this "tell" you what is possible, and not some antiquated belief that you picked up from your Great Uncle Mike.

Vincent Harris is the author of The Productivity Epiphany. Vince long ago realized the wisdom in having a passive income stream through affiliate marketing. http://www.PeaceOfMindMoney.com

Make a Small Fortune As a Visitbank Affiliate

I'm often asked what the easiest way to make money online is if you don't yet have a product of your own, or, if you just don't think you have what it takes to create a good product. My answer is always the same: Become a Visitbank Affiliate.

Visitbank has a nearly unlimited listing of digital products from just about any category or topic you can imagine. Every product you see is available to you for making a handsome income online. Why are the creators of these products so eager to pay you a commission for promoting and selling one of their products?

The answer is rather simple. The more people they have promoting their product, the more money they make, even when they are paying up to 75% commission. Imagine that someone purchased a product that someone else has created that has a price of $100, and you are paid $75 for each sale. This very structure is what has made it very possible for common everyday folks like you and me to make a significant monthly income online.

Think of it like this. What if you went to a Wal-Mart and really liked the way they did business, so you started telling everyone you know about your wonderful shopping experience there. Then, every time someone you told makes a purchase there, you are paid up to a 75% commission. You didn't have to create the product. You didn't have to ship it. You didn't have to place it on the store shelf. All you had to do is tell someone about it and BOOM; you are now being paid for simply making them aware of the product and good service.

This is kind of how affiliate marketing works. Someone labors for weeks-even months- to come up with a great digital product. They test it, they refine it, they test it again, and finally, it's ready to go public. When it does, you have the opportunity to immediately profit from a product that is already a proven winner. How much easier does it get.

I urge you to consider creating as many streams of income as you can, and a good place to start is with an online business as an affiliate marketer.

Vincent Harris is a Body Language Expert and the author of The Productivity Epiphany. http://www.VinceHarris.com

http://www.PeaceOfMindMoney.com

Make Money Online - 6 Reasons Why You Should Start an Affiliate Marketing Business

1. Get Started Instantly For Free.

You can start an Affiliate Marketing business for free you don't have any large expenses that could stop you getting started.

Why pay for things like:

* Credit Card merchant facilities
* Web Hosting
* Advertising
* Or even a product to sell

You can get all this for free and start building your affiliate marketing business today.

2. No Need To Create Your Own Product.

One thing that most people have trouble with when wanting to start a business is what products or services they will offer. When they decide on what type of product or service to provide they still have to do a large amount of work to get it all ready before they can even start their business.

With affiliate marketing someone else has already done all that work for you so instead of spending months to get a product or service ready you can start working towards getting customers and making money right away.

3. You Don't Have To Quit Your Day Job.

When starting most businesses you have to quit your day job to work your business and that creates a lot of pressure on you to succeed from day one.

The fact is it can take time for you to learn what you are doing and to start seeing the results you want and without a source of income you would be forced to give up and quit before you even got off the ground.

You can build your affiliate marketing business in your spare time and when you start getting the results you want you can quit the day job and enjoy more free time doing the things you want to do while still building your business.

4. Do What You Enjoy Doing Most.

Most people work doing things that they don't enjoy just to pay the bills and that really is unfortunate.

When starting your affiliate marketing business you should look for products or services to promote that you would enjoy learning more about and would love to write articles on or answer questions in forums and be happy doing it just for fun even if no money was involved.

The fact is that if you are trying to build a business doing something you don't like then you will not be able to stay motivated when you start to struggle or hit an obstacle you need to overcome.

5. No Need To Deal With Customers

Lets face it customers can be a pain in the butt and in todays world of the customer is always right who wants to deal with unreasonable people that no one could make happy.

When you do affiliate marketing you are promoting a product or service provided by someone else and they do all the work of supporting the customer and answering their questions and you get paid for referring paying customers to them.

So when you get people to the site and they purchase the product and don't know how to use it then it's not your problem to deal with. That is all handled by someone else and you get paid for sending them the paying customer and can just sit back and relax because you have already been paid for a job well done.

6. Do The Work Once Then Get Paid Over And Over.

As an affiliate marketer you get paid for referring paying customers to a product or service. This can be done for free by writing articles on the subject or answering questions in forums.

When you do this people will be interested in who you are and what you do and will check out what you are recommending because they found your article or post in the forum useful.

Because they are interested in what you are promoting they may purchase the product or service and if they do you get paid for it.

But because the articles and forum posts stay on the internet pretty much indefinitely people will come across your articles and forum posts long into the future so the time you spent writing that information will pay off over and over long into the future.

So How Do You Get Started?

The affiliate marketing site I use is http://www.visitbank.com they have over 10,000 products to choose from in pretty much any area you can think of and they will only allow high quality products to remain on their site so you know that you are promoting products of high quality that people will want.

You can even promote multiple products if you want and all the money you make is on the one account so it's easy to keep a track of what you are doing.

If you enjoyed this article then go to http://www.makehomebusiness.com <http://www.makehomebusiness.com/ to learn more about how

you can build a successful internet business from the comfort of your own home.

Anthony Irwin is an Internet Business Entrepreneur building multiple Internet Businesses for fun and profit. If you wish to find out more about the Learning Resources Anthony Irwin recommends to quickly kick start your own Internet Business and begin building a successful money making business then go to http://www.makehomebusiness.com

What Public Speakers Need to Know About Affiliate Links

As a public speaker, you make much of your income selling information products, and not just your own. You sell other people's books. Online, where your business is moving, the equivalent of selling other people's books is using "affiliate links."

An affiliate link leads to a vendor's site. You put it on your webpages or in your e-mail. If someone visits on that link and makes a purchase, you get a fraction of the selling price. You use affiliate links to make money indirectly from your information: You give away information to attract visitors. You get paid when they visit through to buy somebody else's product. The fraction of the sales price varies from 4%-6% at Amazon to more than 50% at some of the high-paying affiliate programs. Some affiliate programs give you a one-time payment. Some pay you a fraction of recurring charges.

Related to affiliate links are Google AdSense ads. Whereas affiliate links are part of a three-way relationship between you, the customer and the vendor, AdSense ads are part of a four-way relationship. You attract customers to your webpages by giving them valuable information. You allow Google to place ads on your page. The vendor pays Google when people visit through those ads. Google pays you a share of the price per visit. Unlike affiliate links, you don't get to choose what ads appear on your page. Google examines the contents of your page to decide what ads are most appropriate.

Why should you care about affiliate links? Income. They can possibly bring you a lot of income. Moreover, if you put up hubs (pages at Hubpages) or lenses (pages at Squidoo), you will automatically get AdSense ads inserted. You should make yourself familiar with them.

You should not, however, use them on all of your webpages. You should never use them on your pitch pages or your squeeze pages: you don't want people visiting off those pages except to buy your product or to give you their e-mail information. You cannot use them directly in e-zine articles. Resource boxes are not allowed to contain affiliate links; although they can link to pages that do contain affiliate links. You may want to use some affiliate links in your mini-course, blog or e-zine -- that's one of the way to make money from them. You can also include affiliate links in e-books and online courses.

When should you use an affiliate link? My rule is this: if I'm going to recommend some product or service anyway, if I believe it will be of value to my reader, and if the vendor is offering an affiliate program, I'm no fool, I'll use the affiliate link. I will not recommend something I don't believe in just because it has an affiliate program. I will not fail to recommend something I do believe in just because it does not have an affiliate program. And overall, I recommend what I prefer, and I strongly prefer things that are free. You'll have to make your own ethical decisions.

Beyond the ethics, there is a practical consideration: You only make significant money out of repeat sales based on long-term relationships. You will gain or lose respect based on the quality of the products and services you recommend.

One extra thing you should know about affiliate links is that they are often quite long. When an affiliate link is broken between lines of an e-mail, it ceases to function. To get around that problem, go to tinyURL.com and, for free, convert the long link into a short one. This also allows you to cloak affiliate links, preventing people from removing your affiliate identification, which people seem to enjoy doing.

A way you can get in on an affiliate program is to go to the website for the product or service you wish to recommend and look for a link labeled "affiliates," "associates," "partners," or something similar. It may be hidden at the bottom of the webpage in tiny print along with links to other sections of the website.

Use affiliate links where you think they are appropriate. Affiliate links provide some people with fortunes, but even if they don't do that for you, they may give you a few extra income streams.

You're invited to get more information on how to use web affiliate programs <http://www.moneymakingideaonline.info/L6_AffiliateLinks.html> or sign up for a free e-learning course for public speakers on creating online income streams <http://www.moneymakingideaonline.info/Speakers/> . These were prepared for Speakers In Colorado by Prof. Christopher, a seminar leader and public speaker.

Increasing Your Affiliate Referrals

So you've got yourself signed up for a new two-tier affiliate program and are excited to start promoting the program to increase your earnings. How are you going to go about drumming up interest in your referral link? The following are a few strategies to help you generate referrals (and revenue, of course!) over the long haul:

Think about search engines when you're structuring your blog posts. Make sure you have relevant keywords in your title. This is absolutely essential. Especially if you're in a really specific niche, make sure you use relevant keyword phrases through your post.

But . . . remember the quality of your posts is more important. Stuffing your posts with keywords makes for stiff, artificial-feeling prose that no one wants to read. Not only is it ugly, but it seems fake. People these days are super-saturated with information. If your readers can tell that you're a real person that has real knowledge they're going to trust your post more, be more likely to visit on your referral link, and are more likely to link to your post.

And those links are at least as important as keywords. Having people linking to your post not only helps readers of other blogs find your post, it also increases your standing in the Google rankings which pushes you towards the top of a list of search results.

Timeliness is relevance. If a new offer has just come out, you've signed up for it and you're trying to promote it for the referrals, if you can write the first review or one of the first reviews of it, you're going to register as the most relevant content on the subject when people search for it. Why? Simply because you're going to be the only content for "Widget Affiliate Offer Review". This has a multiplier effect, since you will be many people's first, and if you're good, authoritative source of information about the offer.

Remember authenticity and objectivity are your best selling points. This was covered a few points up, but bears repeating: everyone is tired of sales pitches, marketing language and all that other nonsense. Web-saavy folks like the affiliates you're trying to refer are cynical and impatient. Give them honest information, pros and cons, and mastery of the information, succinctly and in style, and you're going to go the better part of the way towards selling them on the referral.

About the Author: Peter Ryan is an online marketer and representative of Adapp Solutions, Inc., providing online advertising <http://www.hasoffers.com/> and affiliate marketing software <http://www.hasoffers.com> solutions.

Affiliate Marketing - Take it to the Second Level

So you have got yourself set up as a successful affiliate. You have got a steady stream of revenue coming in from the offers posted on your site. You could sit back and rest on your laurels and just keep doing what you are doing, but what if you want to keep growing? Where do you go from here? There are many ways to increase your revenue stream, but here we will be discussing taking it to the next level - literally. Two-tier marketing is an excellent way to augment your income as an affiliate.

So what is two tier marketing, exactly? Well, what you've been doing up until now - publishing content, serving merchant offers on your website, and earning a commission for each user action - that is single-tier marketing. The scenario is pretty straightforward, you attract traffic to your site and, by extension, to the merchants you are partnered with, you convince your users to buy the merchant's product or signup for their service, you get a cut.

But think about the following scenario: You strike up a correspondence with someone working in the same space as you, and you turn them on to a very good merchant. That merchant sees an increase in traffic and activity and earns more profit, the person you referred to them is making good money from their commission. But none of it would have happened without you.

This is where two-tier marketing comes into play. You've done work for the merchant and in a single tier system, it's good karma and nothing else. And while karma may be good, we all got into business to earn a living. A two tier system means that you refer someone else to the merchant so that they can become an affiliate. You get a commission on everything the person you referred sells. It's a win-win-win situation.

Commissions for signing up affiliates are never as big as the primary commission, so it's not a good idea to try to make this your main revenue stream. A decent commission would be fifteen percent on the first tier and five percent on the second tier. Of course this will vary greatly depending on the market.

Like everything else in the exciting world of affiliate marketing, there's far more to a two-tiered affiliate system, but this has given you the basics.

About the Author: Peter Ryan is an online marketer and representative of Adapp Solutions, Inc., Adapp is known for the development of HasOffers <http://www.hasoffers.com> affiliate software, providing affiliate networks <http://www.hasoffers.com> with the tools they need to run an efficient and profitable online business.

The Positives of Being Taught Internet Marketing by a Mentor

There are several positive sides to hiring an Internet marketing coach who can guide you through the several features of marketing techniques. When you interview a coach before you sign them up then you are on the verge of making it big in affiliate selling. A good internet coach will help you avoid the mistakes which some marketing beginners make on internet-you don't have to lose your hard earn money through common mistakes.

A great teacher will not only teach you the nitty-gritty of the business, they will also give you the practical knowledge of what you need to succeed. They will teach you how to replicate what they have successfully accomplished. Though a good internet mentor will cost you some extra money, you don't have to worry about it compared to the amount you will gain in terms of traffic generation and general sales on your marketing skills.

One advantage that internet marketing mentors have is that they understand what motivates a potential client and knows how well to handle different potential customers that will sign up or buy your products and services online. A reputable Online teacher will always have a successful plan which he follows - this plan has been studied and used for years and it has a tremendous probability to generate your desired result at all times.

An ideal candidate helps you design an aggressive blog, press and other tools to launch your products and services at the top, you will have access to live interactive training sessions online, and you will get services such as Personal development and marketing training, Comprehensive mind set training, comprehensive internet business matching services, and comprehensive suites of marketing tools.

The mentor will help you build a professional image by creating an online business profile, he/she will also help you market your business using your profile to promote press, blogs, press, audio, and video. They will also connect you to other professionals based on the geographical region, Industry and common shared interests. If you have tried several techniques and they have not worked for you, then it is time to seek the services of a mentor and you will be surprised at how things will change for the better in your sales programme - it is believed that more than 90% of failures recorded were from internet marketers due to the lack of knowledge using marketing tools.

For all of the latest products, news, and case studies on affiliate training personnel please visit Work From Home <http://internet-marketing-2009.blogspot.com> and Money Making Review <http://www.maverickmoneymakerssecretclub.com>

Why Do Publishers Join Affiliate Networks?

If you're just dipping your toes into affiliate marketing it might make sense to find a few merchants with affiliate programs and products that mesh well with your current website. If you're looking to do a big cannonball into the fecund waters of affiliate marketing, however, you might want to seriously consider an affiliate network.

A what? Affiliate networks act as a sort of middle-man between publishers and merchants. Affiliate networks gather networks of merchants with affiliate programs that you, as a publisher, can freely choose from. Joining an affiliate network is usually free for the affiliate or publisher so you can sign up for a few and compare their offers and see what fits best with your goals.

Why bother, if I already have some good offers on my site? Joining an affiliate network gives you a number of advantages, including:

Pre-screened vendors. Networks tend to screen the merchants they accept for the program (they often screen publishers as well) so you know that you're getting offers and products from companies that have been vetted for you. Having confidence in your products will make them easier to sell.

Consolidated payments. If you're working with a bunch of different merchants on your own, it can make tracking your payments and other bookkeeping tasks a real chore. Affiliate networks generally take payments from merchants and consolidate them for you into a single check. How often you get paid varies by network, so make sure you check the terms of service, but you will get all the money you've earned in one sum, at a predictable time.

Analytical tools. Many affiliate networks offer tools to help you collect and analyze data about your customers' activity. Since so much of your success as an advertiser depends on your ability to target your content and product offers to the proper audience, having as much data as possible on how people user (or don't use!) your site can be a very valuable thing indeed.

Ease of finding offers. Since the business of an affiliate network is to find vendors and match them with publishers, they've done a lot of the heavy lifting for you. You don't have to spend hours and hours on the web tracking down affiliate programs. The network will have a list of offers you can choose from on their site.

While it's certainly not necessary to join an affiliate network in order to make money at affiliate marketing, in many circumstances it can make your life much easier. And since they're free to join for publishers, you really have nothing to lose.

About the Author: Peter Ryan is an online marketer and representative of Adapp Solutions, Inc., providing online advertising <http://www.hasoffers.com> and affiliate marketing software <http://www.hasoffers.com> solutions.

Building an Affiliate Marketing Website From Scratch

Have you been making a little bit of money with some tentative affiliate marketing offers on your current website but are looking to get serious? Are you looking to start from scratch in affiliate marketing? Either way, you're probably looking at starting a brand new site as either your first one or as an expansion of your properties. One of the many keys to success in affiliate marketing efforts is targeting your work properly. The following are some ideas about how to zero in on a topic for your new site that will help make money. But however you decide to do it, keep in mind that you need to target your site very specifically.

Do what you love. The most obvious topic for a new blog or website is something that you love and that you are already well versed in. If you are already an expert in a topic, or are interested enough to become and expert, you will be able to create lots of detailed, credible content, and you will stay motivated enough to do so. The problem here is that your interests may not jibe well with what's going to make money. Still, this is a very good way to go about picking a topic.

Know your audience. Alternatively, before you decide what you're going to sell or what format you're going to use, you could decide on a specific target audience. Research them - what products they buy, what magazines they read, what websites they frequent. Get as specific as you can. Once you've got all of this information you can begin to find the right merchant offers, develop the proper content, get linked on all the right blogs. The downside here is the possibility that you're not necessarily going to be as capable of or motivated to create really high quality content on a regular basis.

Follow that buzzing sound. Especially if you're prepared to move quickly and get started right away, you can make it your business to become an expert about a hot topic of the moment, like electronic books. Since there's already a lot of background interest in the subject, you're likely to be able generate significant traffic and sales. There's a big if here, though. You need to be a vociferous trend watcher and you need to be prepared to move fast to become an expert in a new topic, set up a site, and move. After all, the buzz around a topic in our internet age doesn't always last all that long.

There are, of course, many ways to target your blog or website, but these are just a few ideas.

About the Author: Peter Ryan is an online marketer and representative of Adapp Solutions, Inc., the creators of HasOffers, affiliate software <http://www.hasoffers.com> .

Affiliate Marketing 101 (the Basics)

Good day,

I'm going to go through the basics of Affiliate Marketing today, something that is done by many people making money online. It's not the only way, but I should tell you it's one of the easier ways to make money online, which is why so many people simply love it!

If you don't already know what affiliate marketing is, it simply means you market and promote someone else's existing product and get paid a percentage of the price as a commission . There are several good companies that you can go to and find products to sell - such as Visitbank.com, PayDotCom, Commission Junction, etc. They all have their pro's and con's, but I prefer Visitbank myself so that is the one I will use as an example here. (Note: check the others out too, don't blindly follow me or anyone else's dictate - be your own person and weigh the benefits that you prefer).

One of the most important things to consider when selling a product as an affiliate marketer is to choose your product wisely! I can't emphasize that enough. First of all you want a product that you at least know something about, and even better yet consider yourself a fan of (or consumer, if it's a product) the product so you can honestly promote it. Believe me the sincerity will show through when you must create sales copy or write articles for this product. The other important thing to consider when choosing a product is find a product that has a "built-in" demand already! You can't force people to buy something they don't want or need, so choose carefully what you will promote. They way to do this is to find the products "gravity" once you log into Visitbank, which is a number ranging from zero to several hundred depending on the popularity of the product at the moment. This number changes frequently, so choose one that is at least 80-100 so you know there's a market ready to buy. This will make promoting the product much easier!

Once you have chosen a product you like, that has a somewhat decent gravity, you're almost halfway there! Go to the "pitch page" of the product and make sure it appears to be a professionally done site, and if so, signup for the product. Once you sign up for their affiliate program you must create what's called a "hop link" - which can be done easily by visiting on the "create hoplink" link in Visitbank for the product you have chosen. This will open in a new window, and you simply copy and paste this link into a text document. The format will be like this: http://xxxxx.myproduct.hop.visitbank.net (where xxxxx is your visitbank ID, and the myproduct is the visitbank ID of the product you are selling). Of course in order to get your Visitbank ID (also called your "nickname") you must sign up with Visitbank first. This costs $50, but it's well worth as you will soon be a wealthy internet marketer, right?

Now comes the part where you must learn a little bit about Internet Marketing - sounds tough but you don't need a big Einstein brain for this, really! Once you have your affiliate link, you need a way to get the link in front of as many eyeballs as possible, preferably through your website. You can either: 1) buy a domain name relevant to your product, and forward this name to your affiliate link or 2) buy a domain name, setup a website, and start getting the content you need to provide value for your visitors. Now these ways both will work, so I'm not going to pontificate over the virtues of either one right now. Suffice it to say you have to do your own homework and decide which is best for you!

Either way you need traffic to the domain, and the ways to do that are varied - PPC advertising is the easiest, but can be very expensive. Writing articles and posting them on Ezine sites is another way which takes more time, but lasts much longer! You can also start up a blog, and write blogs that not only promote your product but have text links that will help you get traffic from the search engines. The best approach I've found is to do a combination of several ways so that you aren't relying on one source for your traffic. However you get the traffic, you can't make money as an affiliate marketer without it so become an expert on this part of internet marketing. If all of this sounds a bit foreign, check some other articles that myself and others have written here and other ezine hubs, and learn as much as you can. Of course I have other articles and posts on my blogs, check them out and learn more!

The fact is, if you can get people to visit on your link you will make money. And that is the bottom line!

I'm being privately coached by an online multi-millionaire. Are you?

Visit making money online <http://www.truemaverickmoneymaker.com> and find out more!

Building a Residual Income Using Affiliate Programs

Residual income is like collecting royalties because you get paid over and over again but you only do the job once. It is one of the best ways to leverage your time and efforts. It's also referred to as recurring income and it's definitely a cool concept once you grasp it and understand how to use it to your advantage. Usually people don't think of affiliate marketing as a means of creating residual income but in reality that's the furthest thing from the truth. Here are a few ways to build residual income using affiliate programs as your vehicle.

1. Develop multiple websites and earn money every month on autopilot. There are people out there making huge amounts of money from websites that they don't even frequent anymore. These sites generate traffic, and create commissions through affiliate sales, because of work they've done in the pass. A good way to do this is by choosing multiple niches in affiliate programs. By doing this you can make money on the internet selling all kinds of products. Also, usually affiliate programs are very affordable and a lot of the work associated with operating your own business are eliminated.

2. Market residual income programs that charge a membership fee. For instance, their are training programs on the internet that bill on a recurring basis, and everytime that customer is billed you receive a kickback. Over time these recurring charges can really amount to something. Website hosting is another excellent affiliate program because anyone wanting their own personal site will have to pay for hosting and they've got to get it from somewhere and that somewhere may as well be from you.

3. You can also market the two tier programs as well. These programs pay you commissions on all of your sales and they will also pay you on all sales made by your organization. By concentrating on duplicating your efforts and building a strong team eventually you will be able to run on autopilot, although I don't recommend that you ever stop prospecting.

4. Finally, you can create your own products and let other affiliates sell them for you. For instance a good example of this is creating a informational e-book that solves a problem and you can sell it on visitbank. Initially, it takes time and a lot of hard work but in the end you will be glad that you did because it will free up your time and you really can't put a price tag on that.

Ronald Reynolds is the owner of Mission Success Biz and writes on a variety of subjects. To learn more about starting your own home based business earning 6 streams of income visit http://www.missionsuccess.biz

Affiliate Marketing Tips - How to Select a Good Visitbank Product

If you are looking to get involved into affiliate marketing then I am going to tell you one place that you need to get familiar with and that one place is Visitbank. Visitbank is that largest affiliate network for digital downloadable products. If you are looking top get a taste then you can go over to Visitbank and select a niche and start promoting that product via your affiliate link

Every time someone makes a sale through affiliate link you make money. You make a commission. Now the product that you pick to promote needs to be sure to have at least a commission of over 17.00, This way it makes it much more of a value to you when you make a sale.

This is how you are going to make sales

Driving traffic- Driving traffic means that you need to send people to your affiliate link. When you send more people there you will make more money

Building a list- You need to build a list of prospective buyers, How you build a list is buy using a squeeze page to send your prospects to before you send them to your affiliate link. When you send them to your squeeze page you need to grab their attention and give them something away for free. Think about, people don't like to walk away from things that are free. I know that I don't

This is the best way that you can get started making money online with affiliate marketing.

Another tip that you can use to select a good Visitbank product is to buy the product yourself. Make sure everything works with the links and read through the product.

This is one way that you can see if you would like to promote the product

Dennis White is an expert internet marketer and the founder of the Video Blog Cash System, He has proved that he can teach people how to make money online in 30 days or less and you can learn now today here at http://www.videoblogcash.com

3 Affiliate Marketing Strategies - Do Something Today!

People get caught up in the get rich quick mentality and jump from idea to idea. Terrified they are going to miss the latest trick and not make a million dollars overnight. Here are some ideas that you can start to apply today.

Affiliate Strategy One

Visitbank is a great place to start finding products to promote. The products here are "downloadable". Here you will find over 10,000 products and services to choose from! Choose a niche product that your familiar with, for example, if your into home repair start with that.

Once you have your product, decide what affiliate traffic generation technique your going to use. At the bottom of this article I have a great coaching system that I'm giving away, it works really good with visitbank products.

Affiliate Strategy Two

Commission Junction is a perfect place for affiliates starting out. They have a lot of "physical" goods to promote. You can sign up with eBay's affiliate program there and start promoting the goods on auctions as an affiliate.

You could use this method of picking your product with article writing. There are tons of ways to advertise your physical products online. Search Google to see what is selling, or eBay for that matter.

Affiliate Strategy Three

Another great way to start getting affiliate revenue is CPA offers. Meaning cost per action, you can get paid for just having someone entering their email or zip code. You can easily replace your income very fast with this strategy.

Start a blog or get an account with a social media site like Facebook, and promote there.

Do Something!

That's right, do something! A lot of people fail because all they do is jump from one product launch to another, "Mr. Guru" is selling a new product so you get bombarded with all these ways to make money.

Stay focused on one strategy, like this <http://www.affiliateconquerer.com/coaching> one.

Give yourself some time. Your not going to get rich over night. If your looking for some real intense training then this coaching <http://www.maverickclubtrainingclub.com> club will teach you everything you need to know about internet marketing (this is the only coaching club I suggest to family and friends).

So in conclusion, stay focused, pick your product wisely, and do one advertising strategy at a time till you make some money. -Brian

Earn $1000's in Residual Income Every Month With Global Domains International

With the economy struggling the way it is today, many people are looking for additional ways to make money. Their regular job's paycheck does not seem to be stretching as far as it did a few years ago. Many people are turning to home businesses to earn residual income. One way is to earn residual income from home with GDI. If you are not familiar with this term, it is easy to understand. GDI simply stands for Global Domains International, which are .WS domain names that you can sell for an extra income. Everyone who has a business has a Web site, which is where you come in to play.

When you earn residual income from home with GDI, you basically are selling the .WS domain names to people who are in need of a Web site domain name. You can also use GDI to create your own website for whatever purpose you may have. Many of the .com domain names are taken because of its popularity. If the domain name you want already is taken, you may think you are left without a name. This is where you are wrong because you do not have to be stuck with a .com name. You can sell these domain names from home because all you need is a computer.

To earn residual income from home with GDI, you have to refer the program to people. This is easy because so many people are just like you and are looking to make money from home. The more people you refer to the product and the more people they refer, the more money you will make. It is a simple way to make money in today's struggling economy because people tend to do more work online these days. You are in charge of how much money you make because it rests in how much effort you put into selling. You can spend as much or as little time as you want in this.

No support, means No business. GDI has excellent customer support plus a private members discussion board. Whether you want to pick up the phone and call GDI or contact them through the support ticket system, the options are available. It's doubtful you'll ever need to contact the customer support, but they are prepared 24/7 to help you. The GDI member discussion board is a great place to communicate with other members and like minded work at home individuals as yourself. Many GDI members have fired their boss and working full time at home with the Global Domains International Opportunity!

If you are afraid of losing your job because of the struggling economy, consider how you can earn residual income from home with GDI. The Internet market will only increase as people recognize the potential of having a Web site will have for their company. When they have the domain name they want, that only will increase their traffic. By selling them a .WS domain name, they can have the name they want even if the .com name already is taken. Using this program is an easy way to supplement your income when other people are struggling.

You can visit http://www.income4lifereviews.ws or email me at christiankostyo@gmail.com </christiankostyo@gmail.com> for more information about this incredible home based business. My name is Christian Kostyo. I am a proud member of Global Domains International and I have had a great deal of success only being a member for 2 months now. Now Is the Time To Join!

6 Free Methods to Getting Insane Amounts of Traffic to Your Affiliate Program

Social Marketing Traffic

Learning the skills to research and leverage the social media space is a very important part of setting up your traffic system. With Social media, you are able to use microblogging platforms like Twitter as well as online communities like Squidoo and Facebook to grow your outreach and target your targeted markets quickly and easily.

While you are a marketer first, friend second, you want to form a personal connection with your target audience. Here are some of the best social communities to get involved with: Twitter: Friend Feed: Facebook: Stumble Upon: Del.icio.us: MySpace.

Article Marketing Traffic

The concept of article marketing is a very simple one: You write high quality content and distribute it amongst popular article databases and directories online, generating tons of traffic from the back links in the attached resource box. It really is as simple as that.

Think about it, writing a 1,000 articles that don't convert, versus 12 that do, which one would you choose. If you rush your articles without conducting some keyword research and coming up with articles that consist of a solid headline, fluid content and no call to action, not allowing the reader to visit the links within your resource boxes, leaving the article directory itself to find out, you are literally throwing money away.

If these readers fail to follow through, your article was for nothing. You should think of your resource box as a 20 second commercial. What is the strongest message that you can use to motivate your readers to visit on your link?

If you are not sure what you can offer within your resource box, here are a few things I have used successfully for over a year now:

- A Free Report
- Subscription to your newsletter
- A free ebook
- A free sample of your product
- A Free Membership
- A Free Video Guide
- A audio transcript or call

Forum Marketing: Quick Back Link Strategy

Forum marketing is probably the easiest ways to generate quality back links to your website (higher ranking in the search engines), as well as potential subscribers and customers. .Don't burst onto the scene, spamming all the threads "me, too!" responses, because before long your find yourself banned or simply ignored. start off helpful, share tips, resources and information, approach forum marketing as you would approach social networking, by offering help and building your brand.

Viral Marketing: Spread It Like Wild Fire

You've most likely heard of Viral Marketing, but might not really know how to set up a Viral marketing campaign that is likely to go viral, basically being carried from person to person, eager and willing to share your website link with friends, family and online acquaintances. Creating a viral marketing campaign is nowhere near as difficult as most people believe, and can yield an impressive return on investment if you do it correctly. Here are a few simple ideas to help you set up a viral marketing campaign of your own:

#1: Offer Incentives Viral marketing always works best when a valuable product or service (including tangible items) are offered.

#2: Be Incredibly Different If you want to generate a buzz around your website.

#3: Run A Contest Or Challenge One of the easiest ways to create a viral campaign.

#4: Save People Time & Money
Consider creating a package that you can give away with resell rights.

Squidoo, HubPages, Blogs - Instant Traffic

There are three tools that I use to instantly generate traffic to my website, at absolutely no cost, and they are: Hub Pages: Squidoo Lens: Blogs: & Blogger.

Here are a few tips to help you create your first Hub:

#1: Use ORIGINAL content only!

#2: Add modules to your hubpages for additional revenue.

#3: Add links with your keywords within your hub page content, leading to your websites, blogs and landing pages. Add at least two text capsules.

#4: Do NOT post affiliate links within your hubpages

#5: Add fans to your hub and be active within the community and its sub groups.

#6: Encourage RSS subscriptions to build a following and expand your outreach.

Press Releases: Quick Traffic Bursts

Press Releases are one of the easiest ways of getting your message in front of thousands of prospects in your target market very quickly, as well as picking up affiliates and potential JV partners. You want to make sure your press release appears to be news, rather than an advert. The back links that a press release creates is phenomenal, I have seen a huge surge of traffic literally within minutes of the press release being published, and months later, I was still receiving traffic from the circulation of that press release. What you do need to be careful of is that you model your press release so that it provokes an emotional response in your viewers. Your press release title should be no longer than 150 characters in length.

If you would like to find out More and Earn $27,379-$43,768 EVERY week. PLUS be Directly Taught By An Online Millionaire and start earning money TODAY then simply go to>>

http://www.Make-Money-At-HomeNow.com

To Read a Comprehensive review of this amazing Money Making System...

http://www.Make-Money-At-HomeNow.com

Bills Piling Up and Money Just Doesn't Go Far Enough? You Can Change That To-day!

People today are experiencing a verity of problems in their lives like never before. Do you fit in this category? The money just does not go far enough and the bills just keep piling up. Do you know you can change all that? Yes, YOU can, by believing in your self and taking control of your own life! Nothing can stop you once you set your mind to doing something for you.

There is an opportunity to make as much money as you would like by having your own business. The Internet presents such an opportunity right now. People like you and I have a real chance to change our lives by believing in ourselves. I am not a computer genius by any means, but I can see it is possible to get ahead by joining the thousands of people working the Internet. Many who are making exceptional money and never leaving home.

I jumped into it head first. What a mistake that turned out to be. I found out that scams are out there and if one existed I found it. Now I research everything before making a move. I'm finally on the right track and slowly but surely things are coming together. I'm telling you this so hopefully you can avoid making the same mistakes I made. Free is a word that I'I have become skeptical of. If it says free I read the privacy statement and the terms and agreement clauses at the bottom of the page. Find out what they might bill you for next, as "free" does not mean free all the time.

Two ways to work the Internet are find a unique product and promote it yourself or become an affiliate marketer. I prefer the latter as you don't have to sell the product, stock it, handle it, or ship it. You promote your website and send people to the individual's site that handles the product. You make a commission on the amount of business you send to their site. The amount of work is minimal. The bucks can really add up but you have to be willing to take the time to learn to promote your own site and then it all falls into place.

The Internet is here to stay and it will only become more of an avenue for information exchange as time goes by. The time to get involved is Now! Good Luck and never give up your dream!

Did you find this article informative and perhaps a little exciting? Just visit on the link below if you want your very own profitable business.

http://www.Top3ProvenOnlineMoneyMakers.com

How to Make a Lot of Money by Affiliate Marketing Fast

There are many ways to make money by affiliate marketing, and the fact of the matter is that depending on what way you choose to pursue you will make money fast or not.

Indeed, I will skip the discussion about whether it is possible or not to make money by affiliate marketing because there is no question that this is a business model that not only works, it works like a charm and you need little to no money in order to make it work big time.

Now, what are the fastest ways to make money by affiliate marketing faster?

As you may or may not know, there affiliates get paid to promote other people's products which in turn generates a commission.

However, there are two basic ways of generating an affiliate commissions:

1. By selling a product.

2. By providing a lead.

The first one simply involves getting someone to pay for a product that they will receive, usually via download and in some cases physically (depending on the kind of affiliate program you are participating in).

The second one does not involve selling anything, it involves only getting your prospect to provide information (often an email, an application or a trial offer), so in many cases your prospect will not even have to pull his or her wallet to complete the task you will be paid for. This is what is called CPA (cost per acquisition).

As you can imagine, CPA and has the potential to get you to profits faster, because a person is likely to have a lot less resistance to your offer if he or she does not have to pay anything or only have to pay shipping and handling for a free trial of a product they get to keep.

So if you want to make money by affiliate marketing really fast, you must dedicate yourself to mastering everything there is to know about CPA. Maverick Money Makers <http://makequickmoney.info/maverick-money-makers-review.htm> will help you achieve just that faster than any other educational resource.

For additional information about Maverick Money Makers visit this affiliate marketing review <http://www.specialonlinebusinessreviewauthority.com/affiliate-marketing-review.html>

The Newbie Workbook Review - A New Marketer's Dream Come True!

The Newbie Workbook is a new affiliate's dream came true. In the course of 30 days this program will teach you how to set up profitable campaigns that will yield hundreds if not thousands within weeks. The best thing is that to follow this program you won't have to invest your money on anything else but the guide.

If you are new to internet marketing you may have realized by now that every piece of information that could take you to profits seems to be closely guarded by top affiliates. No one has shared their exact technique up until now. Brian Zimmerman, author of The Newbie Workbook, has laid out every single detail in this easy to follow manual for success online.

The Newbie Workbook includes a golden piece of material that is actually worth more than the actual guide: Brian Zimmerman's Journal. In the journal, Brian describes each and every step he takes every day in order to build up his campaigns.

The numbers you see on his sales page are real. I can tell you from experience that you can build up your campaigns from zero to hundreds a week within a month if you follow through with the program.

If you have been dreaming about making money online and you have wished for the steps to do so then The Newbie Workbook is for you! In short words: This program will teach you the step by step process of setting up, refining and maintaining your campaigns from start off to profits...blow by blow!

There is even more behind the Newbie Workbook that you should know. Visit my website: http://bestproductsreviews.info/newbieworkbook to find out how this program compares to other newbie resources that can teach you the exact steps to make money online. Here are the top 3 make money online programs for new affiliates <http://bestproductsreviews.info/newbieworkbook> .

My Online Income System - A Plan That Works

In the past, you might never have considered the thought of starting your own business. You were comfortable, things were going well. You didn't have a real problem meeting all of your obligations, and in fact you were able to save little bit. Then, seemingly overnight, things changed. They not only changed, they changed drastically. It started with threatened layoffs. Then the job was lost. Next, there were bills that you had to lay aside until next month. You never received collection calls in the past but now they are coming in almost every day.

This scenario is being repeated millions of times by people just like you. Some are hitting the streets trying to find a job. That is admirable, and in some places the work is being rewarded with results. Often times, however, there are no jobs available that pay the kind of income you received in the past. Cash is at an all time low, trouble seems like it is here to stay.

Many people are finding help is as close as their computer screen. The Internet is an amazing tool. There are millions of pieces of information ready for you to grasp. You only need a few to get yourself going on the road to success with your own online business. There are free trials available so there is no money necessary at the outset. You can get started and begin watching cash roll in. Before you know it, you will have returns you have difficulty imagining right now.

The My Online Income System is a plan that you can put to work and it will do several things for you while you are in the process. Just by getting started you will find the following:

* Studying the plan will give you a sense of accomplishment. It is important for your own self-esteem to get started so the sense of accomplishment will return to your own mind.
* The system is easy to follow so you will learn quickly. Knowing that your work will add up to results is satisfying.
* Knowing there are many people who have become successful with the program will encourage your own determination.

There are not many programs that bring their own sense of reward even before you see dollars begin to roll in. Obviously, it is money you need, but the sense of accomplishment and progress is vitally important to your own sense of purpose and well-being. Get started!

Another important thing you will notice right away is the positive, determined and helpful attitude of the people offering the program. The system will work for you because every possible assistance is offered to you every step of the way. The only way you will fail with this program is if you fail to work the program. Doing nothing is your enemy. Putting it off is your foe. Continuing to worry about your situation combined with inactivity will surely make your situation worse.

Why should you believe this system will work for you? Here are four reasons you can take to heart:

* Other people just like you have made it work for themselves.
* You don't have to be a computer or business expert to make it happen.
* The field is wide open just waiting for you to join.
* The system has been proven again and again.

This is a system that works and will build you up from the inside while you are learning to put the program to work for you on the outside!

Time is passing quickly and the only way things are going to turn around is if you take the steps necessary to make them change. Do a little bit of dreaming and consider the fantastic results you may have if you just take the steps to begin. You have already found that no one is going to do it for you.

If you are interested in taking a look at three programs that will work for you, visit http://www.currencymoneycash.com/ and find what you're looking for.

Dale Parsons

The Super Affiliate Home Business Model

Ever wondered how you can reach Super Affiliate status and earn massive commissions? You need to be dedicated to your business plan. You will need to master some internet basics and dedicate your time to perfecting this simple home business model...

Choosing a niche market.

The easiest way to find profitable markets is to go to websites like ebay.com, amazon.com, magazines.com. If you do a search for the top 10 selling products or books, you will very quickly get a good idea of what people are hungry for. Once you have an idea of what what people want you can now go off an choose an affiliate program which is related to your niche. You must ensure that the program you choose is profitable and not over saturated.

Set up a landing page.

This needs to be a copy of the original website but more condensed and less informative. All you need to do here is grab the readers attention and get them to make the decision to opt-in. Here you are not actually selling the product but are trying to presell the product, by just recommending the product to you prospect. The sale will be done by the affiliate merchant's website. This is why you must ensure that the website copy is very good. Would you personally buy the product? Are there real benefits?

Drive Targeted Traffic To The Landing Page.

This is a whole other topic on its own and will be discussed in much greater detail later on.

Article Writing is one of the best long-term traffic generators on the internet today. Content is king. The key here is to write articles based on your niche market. Millions of people read and use articles every day.

Press Releases are another form of Long & Short term traffic. This is when your press release goes out to potentially thousands of journalists who may use your story and publish it in a newspaper or online.

The quickest way to get traffic is through Pay Per Visit. This is when you choose keywords relating to your niche and build a Google ad around those keywords. Google then displays your ad whenever someone searches for your keywords. If they visit on your ad you will pay google for the advertising. This can get very expensive if you do not know what you are doing.

Build A List Through Your Opt-In Page.

This is where you capture your prospects name and email address. This is extremely important. You need to start to build a relationship with your list so that you can follow up with more sales. It is important to give something of value away for free like a report or a newsletter or even some video tutorials

Continue Recommending Products.

Once you have all this in place you can simply follow the procedure with as many different products and affiliate programs as you wish.

I hope you have found this resource useful. There are very few steps you need to take in order to set up your Super Affiliate Business Home Business Model. BUT you must master all of these steps in order to be successful in your Home Business, for more information visit on the link below...

My name is Jon Raubenheimer, super affiliate. If you would like to learn more about the complete super affiliate system to massive internet income, go here now:
http://www.myeasyincome.com

What is Affiliate Marketing and How Can I Earn a Living at It?

If you've found this article because you searched the words "what is affiliate marketing" you are probably just beginning your search for a means to earn an income online. So let me congratulate you on your decision to take control of your own future. Tens of thousands of people now work from home from their computer, and many of them are affiliates who are making very good money.

So, what IS affiliate marketing? Affiliate marketing is a form of Internet marketing in which a company has set up an automated way for people to sign up as online salespeople (affiliates) for the said company's website or product. The affiliate gets a website, which contains his or her unique tracking identification code. The affiliate promotes the website that contains their code, and all traffic/sales generated by the affiliate to their coded site, are tracked by the company. The affiliate is paid a set amount for each viewing, or for each sale, that comes through their code's site.

In today's tough economy, when so many people are being laid off and so few people are hiring, more and more people are wondering what is affiliate marketing and attempting it as a source of revenue for their family. And for those who take the proper training to learn the industry workings properly, who get support and advice when needed, and are willing to take the time necessary to build their business, affiliate marketing is a goldmine. There are literally tens of thousands of companies online who are looking for affiliates to promote their products, and online sales continue to grow. Affiliate marketing allows people to run their own online business from home, without having inventory, with very little to no overheard, without having to performing direct sales, and without needing to track contacts or do follow-ups. Affiliate marketing is an opportunity to get creative and have tons of fun while making tons of money.

What is affiliate marketing? It is an income opportunity that is definitely worth investigating further. It is not a get-rich overnight scheme, but it can certainly be the answer to all your prayers and dreams.

Get $1000 worth of FREE business eBooks and software at http://www.wealthy-affiliate-university-bonus.info

Affiliate Marketing 101 - Try Free Affiliate Marketing Before You Pay Google Or Yahoo For PPC

Many people are losing their jobs and looking towards the internet to provide them a new stream of income. In desperation, they begin their new adventure as they sit down at their computer and type in the phrase, "Make Money Online."

Suddenly they find themselves bombarded with hundreds of ads that read, "How to Start an Online Business", or "How To Make Money Online" or "AffiliateMarketing101". For the most part these ads are honest advertising.

Almost all of the programs you see offered on the internet today have made money for someone, at sometime. Although, there is one thing you need to be aware of: The person who made the most money is the one who is about to sell you their "Secret Cash Flow System".

Some, eager to gain financial freedom, will grasp at these claims of internet wealth blindly, with both arms open and filled with the hope of becoming an internet millionaire. It won't be until months later, after a lot of costly advertising with PPC search engines, buying web sites, paying for mentoring, or buying keyword programs, they find the following to hold true:

They did not need to pay 2K for a "Make 9K in a Week" program.

They did not have to join a wholesale club and buy a website to sell merchandise.

They did not have to pay Google or Yahoo for PPC advertising.

They did not have to email advertise everyone they knew.

They did not need to spend hours a day at their computers data analyzing.

And...

Had they not been in such a hurry to solve their financial woes, (diving into a new profession for most), they would have found all the information they needed to start their new business right here on the web.

The online marketing courses that are sold all over the internet today, are meant to be a short cut to the top of internet marketing success. Sadly, most do not get there. They lose ambition along the way when they find themselves actually working, and not getting rich over night. (like the program said they would). Most new online marketers buy the program and shelve it after a week or two of getting nowhere. They find their dreams of internet wealth in the toilet, along with the money they laid out for keyword finders, search engine optimizers, wholesale club memberships, ppc advertising, and mentoring programs.

This is true of over 78% of new online business owners fail. Why do you think that is?

Is it because the wealth programs sold on the internet are scams?.... No.

Is it because the right keywords could not be found?.... No.

Is it because the market is flooded with identical merchandise?...No.

Maybe, (just a thought here), it's due to lack of experience...Let's Think about this in simpler terms and I"ll give you an analogy:

You are a carpenter, a brain surgeon is selling his successful business with over 100 patients scheduled for surgery, you buy it. Two weeks later you have your first brain surgery scheduled. The patient is prepped and on the table, the nurse has given you your scalpel, you look down at your patient and...nothing. You were obviously under qualified and un-prepared!

Guess what? Internet Marketing is also something most are under qualified and un-prepared for!

FACT: The most successful marketers on the web hold degrees in marketing. They didn't buy a program and make a million. They invented the program. This is not to meant to imply that a person with a reasonable amount of intelligence cannot make money online, but unless they have a fat bank account to buy all the available information out there and short cut their way to the top, my advice would be to do some research first.

There are numerous ways the average Joe can find products to sell, sites to sell them at, and ways to drive the traffic there, without paying a dime.

If you are new to internet marketing, spend some time on the internet researching different programs. Read all the available information and apply some of the techniques you find before you start purchasing Get Rich Quick programs.

You may just find you never needed to spend a dime.

If you found this article interesting and want to learn more about free internet marketing, please
Go here <http://affiliatemarketingtips1.blogspot.com/>

Ana Austin is a South Florida native who enjoys writing, horse back riding, and skiing with her family.

My Online Income System For You

The strength of the economy has always been the people who do the work. The value of the economy is every individual who faithfully goes to work every day and completes the task they were hired to do. Although paychecks are dwindling and people are losing their jobs, that source of strength and stability stays the same. It still resides with the people. The corporate bosses have never been the foundation. They are the ones who stand at the peak looking down, but it is the common worker who makes things happen. They always have been, and always will be.

So how, you are probably asking, are we going to make it through these difficult times? The simple answer is, the same way we have made it through difficulties in the past. The economy will come out of this mess. People will come out of the trouble and be stronger than they were in the past. There is something about experience that adds up and makes people wiser than they were before. If you've made serious mistakes financially, chances are you won't make the same mistakes again. You know what you did, and now you know how to stay away from the same pitfalls.

For many people, starting their own business is the key to turning things around in their own lives. Success and a larger income may be just down the road if decisions are made to press on and not give up. It is very possible to make money online by using your own computer from home. Currency may be hard to come by at the moment, but things are going to change. If you will do what it takes to be successful and follow the steps leading to results, things will happen for you.

Here are three simple steps you can take to see how things can change for you:

* Read about online income systems on the Internet.
* Read some reviews about the programs.
* Sign up for a free trial and started working for your own success.

A very important part is to personalize your plan. Make your efforts about you. Believe you can do it. Believe you can turn things around for yourself. Don't allow your present situation to determine what will happen in the future. My Online Income System is an avenue you can choose to turn your potential around. Be willing to take a bold step for your own future and see what can happen for you.

Difficult times mean most people have to take action in ways they may never have before. Don't be afraid to try. Others are lifting themselves up and doing better. Why not you?

There is nothing lost by searching. See what is available and find out how to make it work for you. There is something great about people who just refuse to quit and start looking for and creating ways to become successful. You can do it!

Take a look at three programs that just might be the answer for you at http://www.currencymoneycash.com/ and good luck!

Dale Parsons, freelance writer

What to Look For in an Affiliate Program Before Joining One

Affiliate programs are a popular means to online riches. By working as an affiliate for a company and preselling a product rather than actually selling it, one could send visitors to an affiliate website and once the visitor buys something from the online merchant, the affiliate ends up getting a commission, a cut of the price the buyer pays for the product or service.

There is a large number of companies employing affiliate marketing to sell their products. For those looking to earn from an online business, working as an affiliate is an option worth considering. One could get started for no out-of-the-pocket expenses other than of course those for the bandwidth used.

There are many quality affiliate programs on offer. The online entrepreneur is in fact spoilt for choice, having the opportunity to work as an affiliate for an array of products ranging from cosmetics to digital products like e-books and software. What to look for in an affiliate program before joining one? Well, there are a number of points to be kept in mind. First and foremost, one should be doubly sure about the quality of the product he is promoting. He should be proud of standing by the product. That is possible if one has the well-being of the visitor in mind. The significance of due diligence cannot be over-emphasized. Search engines like Google could be visited to get a fair idea of the product's quality and satisfaction level of customers. But be careful-there are paid reviews lurking here, there and everywhere.

The commission could be a factor in helping you make a decision. The rate companies pay varies from 10% to 75% or even higher. Make sure you get your due for the efforts you put in.

Many programs open up for you an avenue for residual income, which means working as an affiliate for a particular product could get you commissions accruing from a particular sale not just once, but time and again. This typically happens in case of membership sites, where you may be paid out commissions for monthly membership sales, and then you keep on getting the commission every month as long as your referral is a member or for the time he keeps using a particular software and pays its monthly fee. This could mean that over a period, your income from the affiliate program grows exponentially.

Which brings us to multi-tier affiliate programs, when it comes to what to look for in an affiliate program. In multi-tier affiliate programs, you earn commissions off not only direct sales, but also from sales made through efforts of your referrals, which adds another stream of income you could greatly capitalize on in the long-term.

How frequent the payouts are and whether there are minimum sales or commission requirements to be fulfilled for you to be eligible to receive your commission is another thing you would want to be sure about.

Quality affiliate programs use a good tracking system, ie. you would be credited for a sale once the visitor has visited a site through your link and makes a purchase at a later date. Many a time, it so happens that the visitor himself is not sure what he has bumped into. After visiting a particular site a number of times, he finally makes a decision to make a purchase, so there you are- that's one of the situations where a tracking system comes handy.

Or some sites even offer the visitor a free guide or newsletter relating to its niche, so that the visitor could be helped in making an informed decision and his visit to the website could be built upon.

Jane has hit upon several smart ways to operate online affiliate business. One of the sites she promotes is http://MyInstantBiz2.tk

7 Things to Consider in Selecting the Right Affiliate Products to Promote

So you've decided to embark on affiliate marketing. Congratulations! There's a good income to be made from this... if you know what you're doing. One of the first difficult choices you're going to be faced with - and this will come up again and again - is how to choose the right affiliate programs to promote. With the thousands of programs being offered, it can be mind-boggling having to pick out which one or which ones are going to make you the income you desire.

Well, let me share 7 factors you should study before making such a decision.

1. Choose a product for which there is a demand.

You may believe you've found the best product in that oxygen-making backpack, but do other people think so too? Is there a market out there for this item? You can do some research on this by going to Overture or the Google AdWords keyword tool to see if there are any bids on keywords related to oxygen-making backpacks. No matter how attractive the product is to you personally, if there isn't a demand for it, then it probably isn't the best idea to promote it. Look for products that are useful to people, that will help in solving some problem they may have.

2. Check how much commission you'll be receiving for the items you promote.

Remember, you're going to have to put in as much work and resources in promoting a low ticket item as a high end product. So determine what commission rate is acceptable to you. Generally, a commission of 50% to 60% is okay. For more expensive items, a lower commission rate is acceptable, anywhere ranging from 20% to 45%. Figure out how much income you want to earn in a month. Let's say it's $500. Now with the commission that you're getting from a particular product, do you see yourself being able to make $500 a month from promoting it? If the answer is yes, then go for it.

3. Is the product accompanied by a good sales copy?

Go to the product's landing page. Is it easy to navigate? Does it call to action? Place yourself in the position of a prospective client. Is what you just read persuasive? Does it make you want to get the product? Are there convincing testimonials from satisfied customers? Good sales copy is very important in getting you a high conversion ratio. You can have a very good product, but if the sales copy fails to convince, then you'll have a difficult time getting conversions.

4. What kind of customer support does the product have?

If you have questions about the product, is there someone you can contact who will answer your queries? It's important for you to be able to get your questions regarding the product answered, as it is essential that your clients be able to do so also. If your clients have a good experience with the customer support of the products they purchase through you, it's more likely that they'll come back to you when in search of other products of a similar nature.

5. Does the seller offer a money back guarantee?

A money back guarantee is sometimes what spells the difference between a conversion and a pass. Clients who are on the verge of making a decision will often be persuaded when they see that guarantee. It's so much easier to let loose of your money when you're assured that you can inspect the product and if it somehow doesn't satisfy, you can ask for your money back. If the product you're considering doesn't offer such a guarantee, think twice about promoting it.

6. What is the conversion rate?

Conversion rate is the percentage of visitors who take a desired action. In your case, the desired action is to buy a product or register to be a member or subscribe to something. If you know the conversion rate, then you have an idea of whether the product makes sales or not. If you can, talk to the affiliate seller and ask him. There are other various methods of finding a product's conversion rate. If a product makes 3 or more sales a day, then you would do well by it.

7. Does the affiliate program offer real time statistics?

It's important that the program you affiliate with offer real-time statistics so that you can measure the effectiveness of your marketing campaign. Most affiliates provide basic statistics like number of visitors sent, number of conversions, and commission earned. But if you're doing a pay-per-visit campaign, you'll want more detailed statistics so that you can modify your campaign if needed. So find out about this matter before you decide to promote the product.

Consider these 7 factors in selecting the affiliate product to promote. They'll go a long way towards ensuring that you make the right choices.

3 Reasons Why You Need to Cloak Your Affiliate Link

Affiliate marketing is just about spreading the word about something and getting a commission from the owner when the good word you put in for his or her product, converted into a sale.

Without planning to promote any product you can nowadays write up a blog about nearly anything fun and hip and there will still be words that you could link to some or other affiliated product. While this could be one way to go, the better converting method is the review concept where you are actively using the product and then review it with all the pros and cons - and of course your associated commission tracking link.

Using your associated commission tracking link as is have one advantage:

- It take less time to load a product page.

To cloak your affiliate link using an affiliate cloaker, free link cloaking service, or by manually redirecting it yourself, means that in effect you add some risk to the link being operable. Since it can now be broken by either one of the two or three sites being down - your site, your redirect site if not the same and the website of the product.

I can think of 3 reasons why you need to cloak your affiliate link - over and above the cons I just mentioned:

1. It makes your links look pretty - maybe not all affiliate links are ugly but some are pretty ugly :-)
2. It stops the common affiliate thief - in a small percentage you profit a little bit more for your effort.
3. Managing your link after a product changed - now this is a killer reason.

Need to cloak your link <http://cloakyourlink.com> ? Learn how to cloak your affiliate links <http://cloakyourlink.com/blog/cloak-your-link/how-to-cloak-your-affiliate-links/> the best way.

How to Launch Your Own Successful Affiliate Program

The key to true success online is in setting up your own successful affiliate program. Using affiliate programs as traffic boosters is not a new idea. The new thought is putting special focus on turning existing customers into successful affiliates. With this you will integrate affiliate sign-up into your sales funnel.

The first thing that must be done is to repeat the fundamental steps used in creating an offer. In order to launch your first product you are going to need the following:

- A sales page product
- A new domain name just for the specific product
- Another opt-in page you can use to capture leads for follow-ups on that product
- Payment processing
- A separate opt-in list within your auto responder account for the specific product.

For payment processing, I recommend most newcomers start out with Visitbank. It is very easy to sign up. Visitbank will charge you a one-time fee to get your page up. Also, Visitbank has a ready-made affiliate program that is automatically associated with your product once the account has been created. This is extremely important, because you want to make it as easy as you can to turn your customers into successful affiliates.

An important point that you will want to emphasize in your sales literature is the great business opportunity customers will have in promoting your product as an affiliate. You should try and make this appear as part of the product itself. Remember you are selling more than just one product. You should have mid-level and back-end products integrated into your sales funnel. This gives not only you but affiliates the ability to earn income on all three levels. Anyone who is interested in your products will also likely be interested in promoting your products for a profit.

You are going to need to create incentive by paying commissions on all levels. You will also want to entice people by paying higher than average commissions. Remember the key here, there is no reason to be greedy, when an affiliate makes a sale you make a sale too...

The other key to remember is creating a strong sales letter. If you are not good at writing sales letters, hire someone to do it for you. You can also copy elements from sales letters you have read that made you want to buy. Make sure your sales letter has all the components of solid copywriting involved

- A killer headline
- Focus on features and benefits
- Great graphics
- Focus on the customer
- Bonuses with an estimated value
- Powerful closing offer and guarantee

You will want to make sure that you follow up with your affiliates. Keep the in your loop and abreast to any new offers or changes in the current product. Remember their success is your success!

Jason Rossi is an expert affiliate marketer who rakes in over $1,000,000 annually via his amazing simple guaranteed profit system. Learn how you, too, can break free from the 9-5 rut by doing what Jason does. Just visit http://www.advancedpromotingtips.com or http://www.guaranteedprofitsystem.com

Easy Money to Make - Uncover the Secret to Affiliate Marketing Part 2 of 3

Welcome Back! In part 1 of this easy money to make series, I talked about researching your niche. Ladies and gentlemen this is the key to your success. 95% of all the problems that business owners encounter are directly a result of poor planning or no planning at all. It's easy money to make online when you find out exactly what people want - "RIGHT NOW" and give them more of the same.

In part 1 of this easy money to make series I gave you two of the best market research tools on the internet for finding great niche markets. If you missed the last article then here are two other sites that you can get some great ideas: Mysimon and Trendwatching. The purpose of these sites is to find out what's hot "RIGHT NOW" and ride the money wave.

The next step in this easy money to make process is keyword research. This is the beauty of online marketing. There are absolutely no excuses for guessing. Everything that you need is at your finger tips. When researching markets online you can find out where people are spending their money. You can find out the exact keywords your prospects are looking for in the search engines. You can even drill down exactly which keywords are making money and which ones are not. So, you're first goal is to source which keywords are receiving a high amount of searches per day. This tool is exceptional and I use it on a regular basis (tools.seobook.com/general/keyword).

Once you get on these sites you can type in the keyword to your niche such as 'golf' and each tool will give you a list of keywords that people are using to find out about golf. **Remember** those people that are looking to buy are specific in their keyword search. Meaning, buyers of products tend to use three or more keywords in their search to find exactly what they're looking for. For example, someone that just did a search for the keyword 'golf' is far too vague. There are too many sub topics under golf to know what that people is truly looking for. However, someone that types in - '6 volt golf cart batteries' is very specific and more likely to purchase that item.

Was this article helpful? If so, watch the detailed step by step videos on the link below to understand how you can become a successful affiliate marketer within 90 days or less.

http://insaneresidualincome.com

Make Money As a College Student

As a fellow college student, I have trouble keeping a part-time job while maintaining passing grades. I'm sure many of you may agree. Like many of you may have already done, I searched for the "Get Rich Quick" websites that many individuals "supposedly" became amazingly successful with. After putting my hard earned money into a couple of these "Get Rich Quick" websites, and eventually losing it all... I began to lose hope..

That is until I discovered Wealthy Affiliate. I had been searching all over the internet, trying to find a legitimate website to make money with. I had finally found the needle in the haystack.

Wealthy Affiliate is not a "Get Rich Quick" website. Or at least not right away. It provides comprehensive and easy to learn tutorials to help you learn how to get the most out of the Internet Marketing Business. There is even a very friendly Forum that can answer any questions you may have. Even if you are completely new to the Internet Marketing Business, Wealthy Affiliate is the perfect place to start.

As far as trying to pay off college fees, with my old Part-Time job, I was making about $150 each weekend. But now I make over $400 a week and I have just started! Even a couple of hours a week can earn you a steady income, without having to sacrifice time to focus on your grades! Paying off those college fees will be easier than ever!

With time and dedication, you can become the next success story on Wealthy Affiliate. Join the thousands of supportive members of Wealthy Affiliate and fill your college life with joy, instead of stress.

For more information on Wealthy Affiliate visit Make-Online-Money-Fast.com <http://make-online-money-fast.com/>

Affiliate Funnel System Review - Is Affiliate Funnel System a Scam?

This newly product is created by Alex Goad and Saj P, both of whom have released high quality affiliate marketing products before. The release of this product has created a lot hype and excitement around the Internet marketing world because of the tremendous success that its creators have achieved before this launch.

1. Affiliate Funnel System Review

This system is an updated version of all the techniques that both its owners have used to generate huge amounts of money online. Since the Internet marketing world is changing every day with new rules and regulation, it is important that all marketers keep themselves up to date with the latest news and strategies in the industry.

2. The 5 Modules of Affiliate Funnel System

This huge course is broken down into different parts, each teaching you an important aspect of Internet marketing. All 5 modules are interlinked and should be studied in order for better understanding of the concepts presented.

3. Choosing the Best Marketing Methods for Your Needs

After reading through the entire course, I have learned several methods of making money with affiliate marketing. It was up to me to choose the one that is most suitable for my budget and time.

4. How Does the Affiliate Funnel System Work?

This system does not just rely on one method to make money. You will not be learning just pay per visit or search engine optimization like how other typical affiliate marketing courses teach.

Instead, you will be learning how to do the entire process of marketing to get the maximum value and profits from them. This involves finding their niche and getting their contact details, either through email subscription or sales. After that, you will learn exactly how to follow up on your lead for the most profits.

Is Affiliate Funnel System <http://www.top-review.org/affiliatefunnelsystem.htm> a scam? Visit http://www.top-review.org/affiliatefunnelsystem.htm to read a FREE report about this Online Income System to find out the truth before you buy Affiliate Funnel System!

How Ordinary People Make an Extraordinary Amount of Money Online - Affiliate Marketing, Anyone?

If you're like me, you probably receive a lot of junk mail into your spam folder that advertises different ways you can make money from home on the Internet. If you're also like me, you probably ignored it or just deleted it.

I was the same way for the longest time, and then one day out of curiosity I opened up one of the emails and ended up spending the rest of the evening reading about Internet marketing and affiliate marketing in particular. It was really interesting reading.

I learned that everyday people with no big-time education, just "regular Joes," were doing affiliate marketing online and making so much money they had been able to quit their jobs to do this full time from home.

So just what is affiliate marketing? It's basically a revenue-sharing venture between a product owner and a website owner, although in actuality you do not even have to have a website because you can use free sites like a Blogger blog or a Squidoo Lens. But anyway, the website owner, or "regular Joe" ordinary person, will decide to become an affiliate of, for example, Amazon.com. So they can then place advertisements in the form of banners or text ads onto their website. Then when anyone comes along and visits that link, and if that person goes ahead and makes a purchase, the affiliate gets a commission.

Commissions range from just a few cents sometimes at Amazon (depending on what people buy) to much much more than that. You can literally make hundreds and thousands of dollars a day as an affiliate. The trick is getting traffic to your website, i.e. people to go there and see your advertisements.

I have been trying my hand at Internet marketing, and my best day so far has been $374.00. I know that it's possible to make a lot more though and many people do. Many millionaires have been made as an affiliate, and it's becoming very popular so the competition is growing greater. However, most people give up real soon so there is always room for someone who is willing to do the work and be persistent. If you are one of those people, you too could be making an extraordinary income working online.

Go here <http://www.makeextramoneyonline.org> to learn how you can earn money online <http://www.makeextramoneyonline.org> right now!

Learn how to make enough money to quit your 9 to 5 job within the next year.

How to Succeed in Casino Affiliate Marketing

Casino affiliate marketing is a fast-growing area of online business which can generate huge incomes with little to no effort after your initial setup takes place. However, there are a few considerations to keep in mind while setting up your affiliate site in order to reap the largest benefits from your new income-generating tool.

Consider your domain name one of the most important aspects to online marketing success. When choosing or changing your name, consider simple and easy-to-remember names like "gamblingonline.com" or "slotsonline.com", versus "winatfive-handpoker.com". This will encourage visitors to keep returning to your site for more information or products in the future, as well as refer others to your site.

The next consideration when developing your casino affiliate marketing program is your site design and content. Web surfers tend to want the applicable information in an outright fashion, versus having to search for it. Simpler is always better when it comes to the design, colors and content of your site.

Content should constantly be updated or added to in order to maintain and increase your search engine ratings, as well as continually offer your visitors something new. This may also help with email marketing programs or new PPC ads you plan to use to find new customers.

As you continually add content to your casino affiliate marketing website, also begin to search for forums you can contribute to on a regular basis. This is a great way to network with those who share your interests, and will position you and your site as an expert source in the market.

You'll also want to ensure your content is specific enough and timely. Outdated information or articles which are too general will only dissuade visitors from actually reading it. This content should also be relatively short and easy to read, as most Web surfers don't want to spend a lot of time reading content word-for-word.

Search for related websites and ask them to exchange links with your site. This may not directly pay commissions like your casino affiliate marketing efforts, but will drive more interested visitors to your site. Sales is always a numbers game, and increased visitors inevitably will increase your affiliate sales!

Finally, ensure you are optimizing opportunities with PPC ads and submissions to the major search engines as well. These submissions and postings may be centered on certain keyword combinations which surfers will input when looking for your site's information and services.

Dustin Heath recommends that you visit http://www.Products-Sell.com to learn how you can start your own home-based business earning multiple streams of income with a Plug-In Profit Site <http://www.HomeBusiness.us> - Complete Money Making Site Setup FREE!

Affiliate Marketing Tips - 5 Tips to Promote Your Affiliate Links For Quick-Fire Profits

Affiliate marketing is one of the best ways to make a bunch of cash online without having a product or even a website. With an affiliate product, all you need to concentrate on is marketing and promotion. You don't have to worry about stocking your products, hiring employees, doing customer support or any of that tedious stuff!

Want to know how to make more sales from your chosen affiliate product? Here are 5 tips for getting more traffic to your affiliate links:

1. Forum marketing. Sign up at related forums and start participating. Create a signature file that has your affiliate link (some forums may not allow this; check their rules). Ensure that you post quality stuff or you will be seen as a product pusher!

2. Blog marketing. Create a blog so you can promote your affiliate product through banners, contextual links and even through list building. Your blog must have high quality content to attract visitors.

3. Blog commenting. This is a simple but killer tactic. Find relevant, popular blogs, and sign up to Google Reader to keep in touch with the latest posts at the blogs. Then get involved and post your link at the end of your blog comment.

4. Ezine advertising. Post ads in targeted ezines to promote your affiliate offer. Solo ads (email promotions that only contain one promotion) are the best because they concentrate only on your offer.

5. Banner advertising. Buy banner ads through a network like Ad Brite or negotiate ad deals with individual sites like high-trafficked blogs. This is a great way to get residual traffic with hardly any work on your part.

Fabian Tan is a well-known Internet Marketing expert and the author of the popular 59-page Report:

"Murder Your Job: How To Build Cash Sucking Autopilot Businesses In 30 Days Or Less!"

Head over to http://www.MurderYourJob.com to get your FREE copy now!

Also, quickly download his FREE "Explosive Traffic System" report that shows you how to generate 10,000+ unique visitors per month at no cost! => http://www.ExplosiveTrafficSystem.com

Affiliate Marketing Secrets - 3 Tactics to Boost Your Affiliate Commissions Almost Overnight

There are hundreds of thousands of affiliates trying to make a sale online right at this moment and many of them are looking to gain a competitive edge. Believe it or not, though, affiliate marketing is not all about generating traffic. Yes, traffic is the most important part of affiliate promotion, but it's not everything. There are other things you can do that can result in massive sales explosions.

Here are 3 must-do tactics that can boost your affiliate commissions almost overnight:

1. Create mind-blowing content. What many affiliate marketers do is they just advertise and advertise without giving any good content away. While this strategy can certainly generate short-term sales, it will do no good in the long run. You want to create content that entices your visitors to come back and spend more money.

2. Article marketing. This is one of the best ways to provide content to warm up your visitors as well as advertise your website! The way to do it is by including the link back to your website in the article's resource box. Once you have written your articles, submit them to the most trafficked directories online. One of them is EzineArticles.

3. List building. Yes, affiliates with big, targeted lists do have a killer advantage when it comes to promotions and affiliate contests. A big, responsive list is an instant promotional device to launch your promotions and make a ton of sales in just days or even hours. The only way you can get this advantage is to do it one subscriber at a time. Start building your list today and cultivate a relationship with your subscribers.

Fabian Tan is a well-known Internet Marketing expert and the author of the popular 59-page Report:

"Murder Your Job: How To Build Cash Sucking Autopilot Businesses In 30 Days Or Less!"

Head over to http://www.MurderYourJob.com to get your FREE copy now!

Also, quickly download his FREE "Explosive Traffic System" report that shows you how to generate 10,000+ unique visitors per month at no cost! => http://www.ExplosiveTrafficSystem.com

Make Money Online With Affiliate Programs - Getting Started

It could not be easier to make money online with affiliate programs; I mean really it couldn't be easier. There are so many of these programs on the Internet that do most of the work for you that it has become a laughably trivial to join an affiliate program and be on your way to making money within hours. In fact it has become so trivial that the market has become flooded with people trying to turn a profit on affiliate sales.

Because of this it is important to differentiate yourself from others in order to make money online with the affiliate programs. The Internet landscape has changed in the last 10 years and you need to put in a little bit more effort if you really want to make the big dollars with affiliate programs. This is not to say it's impossible, in fact it is still quite trivial for people who fully understand how to maximize their potential with affiliate programs to make a lot of money.

The key here is doing your homework and understanding what it takes to be successful instead of mediocre with affiliate marketing. If you want to be just like everyone else with your affiliate sales that's fine, you'll make some money, but you will not make a lot of money. If you want to make a lot of money you need to treat affiliate marketing as your new full time job and put in the effort required to bring in the money.

This means setting regular working hours for yourself and doing lots of research to see what the new trends are an affiliate sales. You need to understand what products are selling, and what products have faded in popularity. You need to work out a system see can quickly post these new products and quickly pull the old products to avoid paying fees on affiliates that you are not selling and get those new affiliates up so you can quickly monetize on them. If this sounds confusing affiliate marketing may not be for you; however if the process sounds intriguing and you should definitely look into it further.

If you want to instantly access a proven step by step guide about making money online <http://theonlinemoneysecret.com> all you have to do is Go here <http://theonlinemoneysecret.com>

Affiliate Marketing Programs - The New Internet Economy

In a very short amount of time affiliate marketing programs have quickly become the backbone of the Internet economy. Most people would say that ad revenues contribute the most to the online economy however these people do not take into account the millions of people who make their money selling affiliate programs instead of ad spaces.

Affiliate marketing programs have one huge advantage over advertising programs when it comes to the average person monetizing their time on the Internet; namely the fact that you do not have to have an actual product to make money with affiliate programs. Unlike advertising models which require you to create compelling content to sell dirt cheap advertising space affiliate programs allow you to sell other people's products for a cut of their profit.

This is an ideal model for people who do not have the time to create a compelling website that is continuously updated with new content. Not to mention the fact that most people do not make very much money when it comes to web advertising. Think about it, how often do you visit on advertisements when you visit web pages? Now consider the fact that most web sites and only receive a few pennies for each person that does visit.

Affiliate marketing programs allow you to break free from the monotony of web site creation and instead focus on the process of finding new affiliates and thinking of ways to market them. It is much more dynamic than continuously updating the same web site and a lot of people find it to be more rewarding; both in terms of monetary returns as well as the enjoyment they get from working.

If discovering new products, working for yourself and controlling your own financial destiny sound even remotely interesting than you should definitely consider, at the minimum, a part and career in affiliate marketing. Its advantages over selling advertising space alone make it something that people looking to make money on the Internet should seriously consider.

If you want to instantly access a proven step by step guide about making money online <http://theonlinemoneysecret.com> all you have to do is Go here <http://theonlinemoneysecret.com>

The Two Tiers of Affiliate Marketing

The process of breaking into the affiliate marketing business is not difficult though it can appear to be rather convoluted to people who have no experience in the field. The most important thing to remember is to not get bogged down in the details. Having a clear overview of the big picture is the most important strategy for success that anyone new to the affiliate marketing business can have.

Once you have a very solid understanding of the general business practices that drive affiliate marketing you can then begin exploring some of the more niche aspects of the field. The good news is that you can spend your entire career as an affiliate marketer never having to delve into any of these more complex topics. It is entirely possible to make a decent living online by just following the basic tenets that you learn on day one. If however you want to earn even more money it is important that you spend the time learning about the latest tips, tricks and techniques that people discover along the way.

Very early on you'll find that people who take the time to learn about niche markets find themselves more successful than people who stick to the basic plans. By researching and exploiting niche markets it is possible to a highly target your potential buyers which in turn drive sales through the roof. Niche marketing is definitely a more complex topic because it requires lots of research; however once you have a firm grasp of the basic techniques it is definitely a field worth looking into.

In fact most of the more advanced topics have to do with reaching customers in new and unique ways that highly target their individual preferences. By learning how to control the scope of your affiliate marketing business you can selectively target customers who are more prone to buying whatever it is you're selling.

If you want to instantly access a proven step by step guide about making money online <http://theonlinemoneysecret.com> all you have to do is Go here <http://theonlinemoneysecret.com>

The Incredible Way to Start an Internet Business

In this day and age, many people are looking for an alternative way to make money. If you want to be your own boss and start an internet business, there are some ways you can do it right and even begun to see profits immediately.

When you are thinking about a business that will provide you with the income you need to survive, you need to focus on what the consumer trends are. There was once a time when many people were flocking to malls each day to make all of their purchases. This trend has changed over the last few years and many people are staying at home to do the majority of their shopping.

With crime rates on the rise, many people are apprehensive about doing shopping in public. With online shopping you do not have to worry about a criminal targeting you in a dark parking lot. Consumers can shop when they want from a secure site. This is very appealing to many shoppers

You can capitalize on this by setting up an affiliate marketing business. Shipping is more available than it ever has been and more cost efficient also. This type of business is very simple to set up and operate and a great way to start an at home business.

Becoming an affiliate is very easy to do once you find the merchant you want to represent. Because there are millions of affiliates programs online it can be overwhelming when you begin to research affiliate marketing opportunities.

One idea is to join an affiliate network which gives you access to multiple affiliates in different categories. For example you can go to Commission Junction and get one I.D. number which will give you access to every affiliate merchant in their network.

Another affiliate network which is very popular is Visitbank.com. They are the largest digital information provider in the world and will give you thousands of ebooks you can sell in multiple categories.

Joining an affiliate network allows you to receive one check as opposed to receiving multiple checks from each individual affiliate merchant. This is much easier for you to keep track of and allows you to grow your affiliate business much faster.

You can start an internet business if you find out what the current trends are in shopping. With many consumers staying home to do their shopping, you can make money and offer a service that is truly in demand as an affiliate marketer.

Paul Jesse is an author and webmaster providing free and low cost opportunities to start an internet business <http://www.work-at-home-whiz.com/blog> . He invites you to visit his website at:http://www.work-at-home-whiz.com

Using Affiliate Programs to Make Money Online

There are a few things you need to do in order to make a decent amount of money selling affiliate programs online. You must first be able to set your website up so that people will buy from it, then you need to be able to promote your affiliate products to people who will buy from you.

Many affiliate companies will provide you with all the necessary tools to be able to sell their products effectively. They will even go to great lengths and provide you with your own pre made website that you can use and set up right away.

I would suggest not to take this route and instead set up your own personal custom website that looks nothing like the pre built one they give you. This will give you an advantage over the other people who are using the pre made website. Totally unique websites will rank higher and get more visitors from Google. You will need to purchase a domain name and find a host to host your website.

This will take a little extra work but your customers will appreciate the effort and you will most likely get a higher conversion rate because of it. Most visitors do not want to see a sales pitch on a product. It works better to put your dialogue and content on your website as a helpful and informative pitch. Put it in your own words and this will make a big difference in your conversion rates as well.

Once your website is all setup, you'll need to go to great lengths to promote your website. This is the only way to get visitors to your website. Many people fail at this aspect and never make any affiliate sales at all.

When it comes to traffic generating techniques, there are literally hundreds of ways you can use to promote your website. It will take time and patience to be able to master the promotion of your website. Once you find which promoting method you are best at, use this method over and over again to market your website.

Once you find your marketing and promoting niche and use it over and over again, you will be able to achieve greater results than by using a hoard of different methods. If you spread your marketing efforts to thin, it will be difficult to get more than a trickle of traffic. Limit yourself to one or two promoting methods that you do best.

It does not have to be difficult to make money online with affiliate programs. If you give it enough time to grow and are promoting your website often, it will be fairly simple to earn money online.

For free training and guidance on how to Make Money From Home <http://www.livelifetothefullest.biz> using the internet, visit Matt's website at http://www.livelifetothefullest.biz

Know the Character of Your Potential JV Partner

Before you solidify a potential joint venture partnership, keep in mind some of the inherent human natures that could hinder your success. Joint ventures are a great way to increase your profits and reach new markets. But with the wrong person, you could face heartache and aggravation.

One thing to keep in mind is that people have a wonderful tendency to say, "yes" to great ideas, but some are lousy at finishing or following up on their side of the bargain. If you form a JV partnership, you need to know that your potential partner can be counted on to fulfill obligations set forth in your agreement and not harm your business or reputation.

Nobody Cares More Than You

Remember that no one cares more for your business and its success than you. When you form a JV partnership, your partner's intentions are not for you business to succeed, but for his. Nobody else will work as hard as you on your business, and you need to make sure that your JV agreement is a win/win situation for both parties.

A new joint venture can be exciting for the parties involved and provides encouragement for the successful outcome. But when the week-to-week and month-to-month management of the joint venture reveals problems, either by low revenue, higher expenses, or more work than expected, you can be sure you'll find out the full commitment of your JV partner. A partner with bad character will find ways to bail out or simply profit himself with no benefit to you. Though it's nice to believe the best in people, you may find it wise to have an attorney draw up your joint venture agreement to protect your business interests.

Depend On Experience

If you are on the lookout for a potential joint venture partner, look for one who has had years of experience running a business and has a good reputation for being trustworthy. New business owners and inexperienced entrepreneurs may not fully understand the commitment required in a joint venture deal and can easily be tempted to take advantage of you. Rather than become equal partners, they may turn out to be followers, and you'll be stuck doing most of the work but still sharing the profits.

With someone experienced in running a business, you know they are familiar with business elements, such as sales and marketing, production, HR, management, and even technology development like websites. If you think it will help, even ask your potential joint venture partner to provide references. Call them and ask about the individual's trustworthiness and ability to handle a tough situation.

Be Cautious With Promises

Generally, you want to be careful when making promises to your potential JV partner. It is always wise to sit down with your JV partner and formulate your mutual goals and outcomes. However, be careful of obligating yourself to a situation that could mean more time, effort, and money than you are willing to exert.

For instance, you could determine that your JV partner will handle all print advertising and you will be in charge of all online marketing. Without realizing it, you could end up putting hours of your time developing a website, or hiring a professional to design one. And your online promotional efforts may take a lot more than just updating a website. You may want to try social media marketing, or even perhaps start a blog about your joint venture products and services. All that could mean a whole lot more effort on your part to maintain a website, write blog articles, and find other ways to promote your JV partnership online. Make sure you all the duties are equally divided between you and your JV partner so there are no hurt feelings or dissatisfaction.

Ultimately, you must be willing to trust your partner and take a chance on forming a successful JV. But taking steps to get to know your partner and determine whether they possess the right character that leads to a successful venture can be the critical insurance you need to protect your interests.

Christian Fea is CEO of Synertegic, Inc. A Joint Venture Marketing firm. He exemplifies how to profit from Joint Venture relationships by creating profit centers with minimal risk and maximum profitability. To discover more Joint Venture Marketing Strategies join his free Joint Venture Marketing Wealth Report <http://www.christianfea.com/joint-venture-wealth-report/?a=3> .

How to Increase Affiliate Sales Overnight

Possibly you are struggling to make money with affiliate marketing. Every now and than you generate a sale, but you just cannot make enough sales to really create wealth online. There is an easy fix for this that will help you increase your affiliate sales.

A really quick solution to your problems is just offering a bonus, when people buy through your affiliate link. Think about it for a second. Why should a person buy from you? There are alot of competing affiliate sites promoting the same exact products and programs that you are. What makes your offer special to someone?

If you are struggling to make sales as an affiliate, you need to visit your website as a potential customer. Read over your copy and ask yourself, Would I just whip out my credit card and purchase this on the spot or do I need some incentive? The incentive is your bonus offer.

In order to offer a bonus, you will need to create a new web page. Take all of the benefits and images from your product or program and than start writing about your bonus. Make it good, don't just offer some "Cheesy Free E-book" that was collecting dust on your hard drive. You need to understand that your customers are always looking for the best offer!

How to put together a great bonus:

1. Write a report that helps inform your target customers needs. In other words help them solve a problem or teach them something new.
2. Purchase some software with master resale or private label rights and offer it as a bonus.
3. Jv with other webmasters. You have found a great product that you think your customers would like. Contact the creator of the product and work out a joint venture with them.

That is just a few ways to put together a "Great Bonus." Use your imagination, the sky is the limit. Your customers will love you because you are offering them a bonus of value and your affiliate sales will increase steadily as a result.

By:Chris Peterson
To find the best free affiliate programs <http://www.affiliatefuel.info> to make money online and information all about affiliate marketing <http://www.affiliatefuel.info> , Visit affiliate Fuel Today!

Warning - Affiliate Marketing Newbies!

The fact is that about 90% of all affiliates marketing on the internet will make less than $100.00 a month. Unless you can get really good at the following, you should not expect to make a full time income at it. The following are:

1. Building a good web site that has a very good conversion.

2. Optimize your web site on keywords that are searched highly, but have a low competition ratio. Having good SEO on your web site will bring you traffic and will help get you in the search engines so people will find you.

3. Choosing the right affiliate will be a trial and error effort and learning the right ways to promote them.

There are a lot of people that assume that affiliate marketing is a fast way to get rich fast program. These kinds of people will do very little work and probably only promote a few banners and think that affiliate marketing does not work when they don't make a red cent.

The truth is that it takes some work on your part. The more you devote time on your business, the more you will make. If you are a fast learner and become good at marketing your affiliates, you will make a lot of money. But the fact is that many affiliate marketers are only doing it part time due to the reality that they have a job and personal life.

At the beginning, the hardest part will be the first couple of months. You might get discourage at first when you see your stats and only see a couple of sales, you will probably have some uncertainty if this really works and that all that work was for nothing. The commissions will start to roll in if you stay committed with your hard work and don't give up.

The traffic that goes thru your web site is one of the biggest factor with affiliate marketing. Of all the traffic that goes thru your web site, only a percentage of that traffic will convert to buyers.

The important thing here is to know your visitors, and being able to supply them with the best affiliate product that is going to best solve their problem or meet their needs. If you have done your research in your niche and have a compelling pre sale, which is the ability to put your visitors in the state of mind of being in a purchasing mode, you will have a lot more visits on what you are offering.

You will learn more and more as time goes on. At first, you might be disappointed at the results, but with all your efforts and as you grow as an affiliate marketer, you will see your commission checks increase. Remember that nothing comes easy if its worth having and if being financially independent is worth having then its worth putting in the time.

Affiliate marketing is a great way of building an internet business and making a great income if done the right way. Marvin Z. Stanton is known for his knowledge in the internet marketing and making money on the internet. If you would like free money making resources <http://www.buildyourwebempire.com/Free-Resources.html> or more information on how to make money now <http://www.buildyourwebempire.com> , check out our web site now.

Make Money Online on Autopilot - Discover 5 Surefire Ways to an Automated Income Online

Making money online in itself can be a big challenge (it needn't me by the way). But for those who have success, many are just working no more than a 9-5 job from home. Plain and simply because they do not use using marketing methods and strategies that leverage their time.

In this article I am going to show you and elaborate on 5 methods and marketing strategies that will help you automate your income online. They are:

1. Video marketing.
2. Outsourcing your work
3. Pay Per Visit Advertising
4. Take on affiliates
5. Use viral marketing

Now don't get me wrong, if you're new to making money online then at first you will need to invest time. But it is also important, early on, to build a foundation that insures long term stability. That's when you can set your business on autopilot!

So here they are:

1. Video marketing

This is not only a very powerful form of advertising your products or service but once you set up your videos correctly and they have "Great Content", then people will recommend your videos and you will get a huge numbers of views without you having to do anything. I cannot recommend them enough for anyone looking to leverage time in their business.

2. Use PPC Marketing

You may be doing this already but I want to be sure that I don't give their impression here that you can just set up campaigns and leave them running you will need to check and make frequent adjustments but using 'AdWords editor' this can be done very easily.

3. Use Viral marketing

This again is a very powerful method to expand your business and really does not take up a lot of your time at all.

4. Outsource your work

Don't for one minute think you have to master every skill in online marketing...very few people can. If you are struggling with one particular area e.g. website creation or copywriting then you MUST outsource that work, because it will save you so much time learning, failing, it will relieve you of a lot of stress and they will be doing to better than you anyway.

5. Use affiliates

Taking on a building a good relationship with affiliates is paramount to you growing a large business without it taking on lots of time. Affiliates will essentially do ALL YOUR WORK FOR YOU IF... you help them upfront and give them the best tools possible. I advice to be very generous to your affiliates on the front end even giving them as much as 100% on each sale, you will make more money on the back end.

6. (As a bonus) ...Use an Autoresponder!

I know a lot of people reading this know this already but how could I write this article without including this?

Simply answer...I couldn't!

Using an autoresponder is ESSENTIAL to any kind of lasting success online.

There you have it 6 ways to instantly automate your income online.

If you want more help with learning simple ways to making money online and fast then here is all the help you will ever need:

http://www.InstantMaverickMoneyMaker.com

Safe Work at Home - Affiliate Marketing is an Option

With the world being as it is now, safe work at home is fast becoming a viable livelihood alternative. What was once the domain of retirees and mothers who still wish to earn extra income while tending to the children, working from home has become a phenomenon that everyone wants a piece of. This attractive alternative is slowly gaining wide acceptance in the business world because it offers numerous positive implications for energy conservation, environmental protection, family value formation and of course, worker safety.

Many of these work-from-home opportunities can be had in the internet. Many companies have now turned to the internet for advertising and marketing, as well as selling products and services. Affiliate marketing is an area where extraordinary growth has been observed. As internet use becomes more and more widespread, both in developed and developing countries, the opportunities for increasing sales also increase. Many website owners and bloggers have started cashing-in on these opportunities by engaging in affiliate marketing. Many of whom have made affiliate marketing as their primary source of income.

Another on-line opportunity for having safe work at home is building a business with operations done mainly through the internet. Transacting through the internet has never been this easy and safe as it is now. One has various choices of how payments can be done and received. In fact, major credit card companies and banks have worked out the safety of internet transactions.

Although the internet provides a wealth of opportunities for having safe work at home, many of these opportunities prove to be scams or just do not pay that much. Examples of these rather shady internet work opportunities include those that ask you to take surveys or to be a mystery shopper. Many of these "on-line job opportunities" promise easy money, but they actually have rather complicated processes for you to earn the money that you were promised in the first place. Moreover, there are a lot of websites that offer multimedia materials (books, pamphlets, internet resources, DVDs, etc.) that claim to have the best information on how to earn fast using the internet or have a safe work at home, but the reality is that many of the things the materials contain can be found in the internet for free, and the only one who earn money from these materials is the person doing the scam.

Safe work at home promotes energy conservation. Telecommuting offers opportunities to save on transportation and building utilities. An improved family life is also a benefit of having a safe work at home.

Do you want to learn about the #1 internet marketing program on the internet? Discover how you can begin earning a significant income working at home in a legitimate business - Safe Work At Home <http://Make-Money-Systems.net> .

I have worked from home for over 20 years earning a comfortable living. It was a little scary at first but I never looked back. The best thing is that my future, my income and my employment status is completely under my control.

I never have to worry about a disagreeable boss, commuting and siting in traffic, working on another person's time clock and spending large blocks of time away from my family. Overall, life is good!

http://Make-Money-Systems.net

3 Things You Must Realize - Create Your Affiliate Marketing Mindset

In this article I'm going to briefly cover some reasons why most people fail with internet affiliate marketing. I have given some basic ideas on what I think is the cause. I've included some links that have helped me to make money, and more importantly, mindset coaching.

What Is Your Mindset?

1. Most people have had a poor "conditioned" mindset growing up. What I mean is that they have it blueprinted in their subconscious that they are going to need to go to school and get a good job, work 30-40 years, and hopefully retire with a good pension.

The problem with this mindset is that this isn't proving to be as stable or secure as we were taught.
Unfortunately in this economy.

Breaking The Habit

2. So what we need to do in essence is, re-program our minds to think differently. You cannot succeed in internet affiliate marketing if you keep your old stinking thinking.

Your 40 hour a week mindset isn't gonna work with staying at home making money online. With your job mindset you were taught to trade your time for money.

Trading Results For Money

3. Trading your results for money is gonna be the way you wanna think. Your not gonna be getting paid from an employer anymore. You will be getting paid for your results.

This means you are gonna have to change the way you think, act, and talk. It's going to be the hardest thing you do when it comes to internet affiliate marketing.

The reason why I bring this all up is because so many times I have heard people say that they go through so many products, and do NOTHING with them. It's because of mindset.

Do Something!

That's right, do something! A lot of people fail because all they do is jump from one product launch to another, "Mr. Guru" is selling a new product so you get bombarded with all these ways to make money.

Stay focused on one strategy, like this <http://www.affiliateconquerer.com/coaching> one.

Give yourself some time. Your not gonna get rich over night. If your looking for some real intense mindset training then this coaching <http://www.mavericktrainingclub.com> club will teach you everything you need to know about internet marketing and mindset (this is the only coaching club I suggest to family and friends).

So in conclusion, stay focused, pick your product wisely, and do one advertising strategy at a time till you make some money. -Brian

Your Visitbank Profit Guide

There are many ways of making money online. If you search Google for the term of "making money online", you can find millions of searches found. With huge opportunities for everyone, making money via internet or so call internet marketing has been more and more attractive for everyone.

If you've been learning about Internet marketing, you've heard of Visitbank. Visitbank is a payment processor and affiliate network. When you have a Visitbank account, you can promote thousands of digital information products, collecting a commission for every sale.

If you've created a digital product, you can list it in on Visitbank. The site takes care of paying affiliates and will make sure you receive your payments, too.

Most people who deal with Visitbank started as an affiliate. It's a great way to earn money online and it's very easy to get started. Signing up for an account at Visitbank is a simple, fast process and it's absolutely free. Once you have a membership, you can start promoting products and earning commissions.

In the most basic of terms, affiliate marketing with Visitbank works like is: You drive web traffic to a publisher's sales page. When people purchase the product to which you directed them, you'll receive a commission payment. You are credited for a commission by sending traffic to a specialized version of the sales page, known in Visitbank parlance as a hoplink. Your hoplink is unique to your account, guaranteeing that you'll receive all payments due to you.

When deciding on which product to promote, there are few factors you must consider:

- Gravity
- Refunds percentage
- Commissions
- The Product itself
- Sales page
- Publisher support

In order to get the most out of Visitbank, however, you'll need an understanding of some details. We strongly advise anyone with an interest in using Visitbank to carefully review the sites terms of service, rules and frequently asked question area. You'll find a wealth of information about Visitbank at Visitbank!

Visitbank isn't the only affiliate network out there, but it's one of the most popular. The barrier to entry is low, commissions are high and the site has an established reputation for making its payments.

If you're interested in affiliate marketing or in selling as many copies of your own product as possible, you owe it to yourself to take a long and serious look at Visitbank. It's been a profitable endeavor for many in the Internet marketing field and might be perfect for you, too.

For time being, the author is giving away free report on Proven Strategies That Can Earn You Up To $100,000 A Year. Just go to internet marketing site <http://www.internetmarketingstrategypro.com> to get it.

Maverick Money Maker - Why Are 'Mavericks' Achieving Financial Success?

I must confess I was thrilled and apprehensive at the same time when I was introduced to a program which promised success using innovative methods.

My delight was due to the fact that I always considered myself to be a 'Lone Ranger'. On the other hand I was a bit sceptical in that I wondered whether an individualist approach could produce the results I was seeking.

To resolve my mental conflict I adopted what Rudyard Kipling described them as his "six THINKING men". They are WHAT, WHY, WHEN, WHERE, WHO and HOW.

My first question was: 'WHAT' did I want to achieve and 'WHY'?

I listed down a few ideas:

? An income that would give me greater financial freedom.
? To work from home or anywhere I choose.
? An opportunity that would allow me more free time for myself.
? To be able to spend more quality time with my family.
? To be able to spend more time pursuing my hobbies.

Although I had my 'HOW' I did further research and found a program that provided me with the following:

? A high content quality;
? Was easy to use;
? A high income potential;
? Personalized member support;
? A high success rate.

I was sold on the quality and simplicity of the program and decided to become a member. A further BONUS was the fact that I am able to retain my 'Lone Ranger' approach knowing that I have a Successful Team supporting my business.

The main elements of the program were:

? A step by step Blueprint that will allow replication of the exact formula which is used to generate thousands of targeted visitors and boost monthly income.
? The process is duplicated over and over.

The Risk Free 60 days Money Back Guarantee was also re-assuring. For me it has been a very wise investment.

To REVIEW Maverick Money Makers Go here <http://Fitzgeraldsuccess.com>

If you are serious about creating a Internet Business that sells products in an expanding market, that not only allows the opportunity for financial success but allows you to maintain your pioneering spirit, then the Maverick Money Maker program is for you.

Personal RISK FREE 60 days guarantee

If during the first 60 days of coaching, you're not happy with the program for any reason, you can ask for your money back and you will get a Full REFUND no questions asked.

P.S. As soon as your order is confirmed, you can start immediately as everything is delivered online.

To ORDER Maverick Money Makers Go here <http://Fitzgeraldsuccess.com>

Let me THANK you now for signing up... And welcome you as a new MAVERICK member of the Financial Independent Club.

Affiliate Marketing (Why Do it)

When it comes to making money on the internet there is a lot of how to pages, and gurus bidding for your money. They all claim that they have the secret to make you successful in your internet business. Do they ever deliver on this promise? I have tried a lot of these techniques and secrets, but to no avail. I have went through a lot of money trying this and that. You can believe that I am not a millionaire, at least not yet. Now that that's out of the way lets get down to business. Affiliate marketing why do it, There's a lot of reasons why you should or should not get in this business. I will only focus on the good because they out way the bad. Let's start with the hours.

You will have to put in some work don't let that get you down. In this business you are your own boss, So guess what you don't have to work from 9 to 5 if that's not what you want to do. Don't think this is a get rich quick kind of business that's not true. You will have to work to make money but you can work at your own pace. But you will need to be very disciplined if you intend to make a living doing this. Next there's the products you can choose from thousands of products to promote with out stocking any at all.

All you have to do is sign up with a company and become their advertiser and promote their products. The commission can be as little as pennies or as great as thousands of dollars, all this depends on what you are promoting. The work is not hard if you can write a paragraph or read you can basically do the work. That's about all you have to do to run a affiliate marketing business, Read to learn all you can then write to promote all over the internet.

Joseph Redding I am a stay at home dad and i make money with affiliate marketing. I founded this site http://www.onlinemarketinginfo.info that gives free info on affiliate marketing.You can learn step by step how to setup a website and run a affiliate marketing business, by watching a video course that i have added a link to on the resources page.

Offline AdWords For Affiliates

AdWords has added a fantastic feature that almost any affiliate can use. Offline ads can work phenomenally well, because there's much less competition offline that online.

Newspaper ads can work very well for products that have wide appeal, such as money-making opportunities, weight loss, financial information, and credit help. You've probably seen those late-night television infomercials that claim you can make thousands of dollars by placing tiny little classified ads, right?

They were very popular for a great many years. Indeed, classified ads can be a great way to bring in sales, especially to those products with mass appeal. A lot of people have made fortunes through placing classified ads.

Of course, it's always been a tedious process to place ads in hundreds of newspapers all around the country. It takes a lot of time to contact all of those newspapers, ask for their circulation numbers and prices, and place your ads. It can also be difficult to track which ads have been run, and when.

But Google has made things much easier with their Print Ads program. You can find information about this inside your regular AdWords account admin area. There are hundreds of newspapers currently available to advertise in.

You can choose which newspapers you'd like to advertise in, the section you'd like your ad to appear in, and the day you'd like your ad to run. You can target specific areas, or you can choose to advertise in many cities at once.

The great thing about advertising in newspapers is the fact that there will be less competition than there is online. Let's say you're promoting a weight loss eBook. If you search Google for "weight loss" (without quotes), you get over 76,000,000 results!

Can you imagine a newspaper with 76 million classified ads on weight loss alone? When was the last time you saw more than 100 or so ads in a single newspaper section, aside from perhaps the rentals or real estate sections? Even the Sunday issue of the biggest newspaper in a major city doesn't have more than a few hundred ads per niche section!

You can get your ad in front of thousands or even millions of people for very little money. Classified ads can often be had for well under $100. Some newspapers may charge as little as $10 for a three line ad. You could place an ad in dozens of newspapers for the price of a single banner ad on a high-traffic website!

By using Google's new Print Ads service, you can get lots of traffic to your affiliate website quickly. You could even set up a website that reviews several competing affiliate products, and state in your ad that you have unbiased reviews of the top weight loss products, or the best work at home opportunities, or whatever you're promoting.

David Cooper's Affiliate Marketing <http://www.affiliateavalanche.com/> handbook will show you how to Reconceptualize your Affiliate Marketing Expenses. In Affiliate Avalanche <http://www.affiliateavalanche.com/> , you will learn how to Strike without Warning to Seize an Entire Niche Audience, while other Affiliate Marketers scramble to get out of your way!

Bob Proctor and His Affiliate Programs

Bob Proctor, a Canadian born motivator has won acclaim around the globe. From Australia to Malaysia, Mississippi to Alberta. Bob, a high school dropout, shows how by believing in oneself, having an optimistic approach towards life and mastering the skill of self motivation can take one to the pinnacle of success. He is a renowned author, counselor, business consultant, lecturer, entrepreneur, and teacher preaching the doctrine of self-motivation, positive thinking and maximizing the human potential.

Mr. Proctor was born in a little town in northern Ontario, Canada. He was the middle child. He performed badly at school. He was dropped out and joined the navy. Later he drifted from one job to another. In the year 1961, Bob Proctor was working in a fire house in Canada. This job fetched him just $4000 annually. He was already under a debt of $6000. Fortunately enough, a friend brought him a book called "Think and Grow Rich" by Napoleon hill. This book brought the turning point in Bob's life. It was all because of this book that Bob made a whooping $175,000 in one year. And later, played in millions. Inspired from Napoleon Hill's book, Bob Proctor started an office cleaning business which brought him his first success. Bob understood the power of self-motivation goal setting. His hunger to succeed grew more and more. Bob Proctor then joined the Nightingale-Conant organization and studied under his mentor, Earl Nightingale. He was excellent in his work. This quality made him rise swiftly through the ranks.

While the Nightingale-Conant organization assumed the forefront in the wide-scale distribution of personal development programs, Bob felt the need to take his ideas and methods to the general public. Bob worked with business entities and individuals to develop strategies that will assist employees at all levels to grow, improve and adapt to the ever changing business environment. Bob Proctor has shared his messages and expertise with numerous business entities worldwide through his live seminars and other published programs. There are several programs that can convince you that you have the strength to do anything and everything, Bob Proctors programs complete the cycle by explaining what you must do, why you must do it and more importantly how you must do it. Bob proctor's seminars and lectures have helped many transform their lives and achieve what they ever wished to.

Bob Proctor also started a successful online affiliate program that can help you make money. You only need an email id or a website. The affiliate program offers product ads that you can display on your website and get paid for every purchase done from your website. You can share the products with your family and friends and earn 15% in referral fees for any purchase made through your special affiliate link. This system provides a two tier affiliate program. The first tier is the one mentioned above. The second tier is, when your people sign up as affiliates to this program, you earn 5% of the purchases made by any of their people. You will be given a unique affiliate login ID and all subsequent links you need to drive your own internet traffic to his site.

Richard is a top marketer who works with top team industry leaders from around the world. He has a passion for helping others achieve their goals, dreams and aspirations. To learn more about Richard <http://www.marketingrichman.com> and his team of global leaders who work from home <http://www.marketingrichman.com>

Affiliate Businesses

Affiliate business has gained a lot of popularity especially in recent times. Affiliate business is related to the internet and comprises of a marketing technique through which the affiliate is awarded for each customer or visitor created by his marketing efforts. Affiliate businesses can be termed as an industry where exist a number of individuals and companies involved in a form of internet marketing.

Internet marketing is mainly done through the network of affiliates, affiliate management companies, affiliate managers, third party vendors and people involved in promotion of the product. According to marketing experts, affiliate marketing often overlaps with other forms of internet marketing techniques. This is mainly because the affiliates bring into usage several advertising methods conventional to both forms. These marketing methods mainly comprise of email marketing, search engine optimization, display advertising and paid search engine marketing. The affiliates also bring into usage several unconventional forms such as reviews of the products and services offered by the manufacturer.

Affiliate business uses a website for driving the desired amount of traffic to the website of the client. This is the reason why affiliate marketing is often also an overlooked technique by the advertisers as they mostly depend upon conventional techniques state above. Irrespective of the less popularity of affiliate marketing it plays a significant role in the marketing strategies of e retailers.

Compensation plans under affiliate businesses: Several types of compensation plans are found under affiliate business. The compensation plans can be divided into various headings.

Predominant methods: This category of compensation plan is the most popular and widely used one. It is estimated that about eighty percent of affiliate businesses out there bring into usage methods belonging to this category. Some of the most commonly used methods under this heading include CPS or Cost per Sale covering more than eighty percent and CPA or Cost per Action covering nineteen percent. The remaining one percent brings into usage other methods like CPM (Cost per Mile) or CPC (Cost per Visit).

Fewer or diminishing methods: It should be noted that less than one percent of affiliate marketing programs bring into uses the CPC or CPM methods. The above stated methods heavily depend upon paid search and display advertising. The CPC methods was very popular in earlier days, but has lost its shine mainly because of the increasing number of frauds related to the method. This is very similar problem to the visit fraud faced by most of the modern search engine in recent times.

On the other hand CPM method requires the publication of advertisement on the website of the publisher which can be used by the visitors. Thus, the amount of commission received by the publisher mainly depends upon the number of visitors directed though the advertisement. This process is different from the Pay per Visit methods as it involves additional methods of generating revenue for the publisher. Thus, the visitor should not only be aware of the advertisement but should also visit on the advertisement for generating revenue of the publisher.

Hi,

My name is Donnie Benda.I am in business for my self because I do not want this problem economy to affect my family so I found a good solid business with alot of support and training to help you be very successful.

God Bless

http://donnieseasymoney.com

How Effective is Wealthy Affiliate?

There are thousands of people out there who are making big money by sitting in the comfort of their homes. Wealthy affiliate is the website that teaches you how to make a big profit by introducing and promoting affiliate products.

This uses Google AdWords.

This is an exclusively feature packed site, providing in-depth tutorials, on affiliate marketing topics. It provides a step-by-step procedure divided into sub-categorical tutorials. For completely new comers to the online marketing, it starts with lesson one teaching the new comers about affiliate marketing. If you are at an advanced stage you can skip off and come to a level that better suits you and your requirements.

Founded by Kyle and Carson, this site is built on a specific structure keeping a specific goal in mind.

The methods and techniques they teach have hands on approach, keeping people posted with daily online forums. Its yearly membership comes at a cost of $360 costing about $29.00 per month, which is rather cheap for all the services provided. The best feature would be the private supervision from Kyle and Carson themselves. They personally log in to your account and keep a check on everything that you're doing and to give you proper directions if you're off track.

The best feature of this site includes:

Provision of templates for the affiliation of your own sites with personalized embedded links.

? Relatively cost effective membership, with a large profit margin

? FAQ section

? latest keyword list each month

? Frequent up gradation and follow-up from the creator's themselves

? case studies, member forums, and tips on how to land your pages

? Excellent affiliate marketing tools and strategies for a better business

? Constant coaching from their side to help you maneuver your investments and return.

In conclusion it is safe to say that Wealthy Affiliate is a resource site that offers a great deal of information and insight into the Online Affiliate Marketing. Considering the fact that you have to go through the variety of information and choose how they implement the strategies in search for online success of your business. Wealthy Affiliate will provide you with a basic framework to learn and build. However it will take hard work and dedication to develop a profitable online business.

For more information, please visit http://www.ryansreview.com/wealthyaffiliate.php

The Fastest Way to Make Huge Visitbank Profits

Everyone who is anyone in affiliate marketing has heard of Visitbank by now. This is usually the place we choose to start our internet marketing careers. It is easy to sign up, easy to use, and easy to get paid. Not to mention those 50-75% commissions.

There are a few secrets to making it big with Visitbank, though. Finding the right niche is important. Generally, if you look for a group of people who have a problem and are hungry for a solution, you're on the right track. And you can probably find groups like that in every category in the Visitbank Marketplace.

It's also important to choose a product that has a sales page that will convert well. There are lots of different factors to consider here, but if it's a sales page that you would buy from, chances are others would too.

Now, if you really want to crank up the heat you can create a blog or other type of landing page and start collecting emails. Just sign up with an autoresponder service and offer a free report or course that has to do with the niche you are promoting, and give it away in exchange for the visitor's email. This way you can continue to market to your visitors and get sales in the back end.

Perhaps the fastest way to make huge Visitbank profits is to get yourself a complete education in internet marketing, so you understand every element of what you're doing. You can still make money without one, but having a blueprint laid out in front of you will get you to your goals a heck of a lot faster.

Be careful though. There are a lot of 'get rich quick' types schemes out there. The very best place I've found that can help you make huge Visitbank profits fast is Wealthy Affiliate.

They are kind of like a university for internet marketing. Lots of tutorials and support. It's just a very complete system, and the best education you'll find. And trust me, I went through a lot of others before I found them.

If you can keep these points in mind when you start out, you'll be making huge Visitbank profits before you know it.

Don't waste a bunch of time like I did...if making Visitbank profits <http://reviewthewealthyaffiliate.blogspot.com> are your goal, go get a proper education first. You can find the very best system here: Wealthy Affiliate <http://reviewthewealthyaffiliate.blogspot.com>

Affiliate Marketing Tips - How to Choose Affiliate Programs That Will Fatten Your Wallet

If you are looking for a part time option to make money on-line fast then you need to look at some of the affiliate programs available over the internet. Most people would ask: How much will I earn through affiliate marketing? The truth is that this will not make you a millionaire overnight but it will definitely pay you well. The amount of money you can earn from an affiliate marketing program will depend largely on several factors like choosing the right program to run with, using eye-catching captions and call to action phrases, and some hard work.

Different affiliate programs have different payouts. You can earn anywhere from 10 cents per visit to $60 per sale. The per-sale payout will vary on the basis of the product being sold. But what type of affiliate programs should you choose? The important thing to remember here is that you should focus on those programs that you will you will be able to do well in. In fact, you can even choose programs that are selling products you have information about or have prior experience selling them from over the counter. You need to analyze your strengths before you choose a program.

One of things that you should never do is participate in too many or multiple programs. This will lead to loss of focus on some of the programs you are signed up with and you will not end up selling any of the products. Hence it is always advisable to focus on a couple of programs and a couple of products so that you can make money online fast.

Fabian Tan is a well-known Internet Marketing expert and the author of the popular 59-page Report:

"Murder Your Job: How To Build Cash Sucking Autopilot Businesses In 30 Days Or Less!"

Head over to http://www.MurderYourJob.com to get your FREE copy now!

Also, quickly download his FREE "Explosive Traffic System" report that shows you how to generate 10,000+ unique visitors per month at no cost! => http://www.ExplosiveTrafficSystem.com

3 Steps to Internet Marketing - Free Internet Marketing Strategy

In this article we are going to cover three basic ideas on how to get your feet wet with internet marketing. I'm going to share some VERY powerful strategies that have worked for me, and the best part they are all free!

Finding A Product

1. Finding a product to sell as an affiliate marketer could not be easier! Starting out I would suggest getting accounts at visitbank and commission junction.

Get into a niche that you are familiar with. For example, if your passion or hobby is golf, start by selling golf related items. Make sure the "sales" page of the product your going to be promoting looks professional.

Affiliate Marketing Strategy

2. Setting a goal strategy is crucial. Don't be jumping around all over the place buying guides on "how to make money online", you will end up broke and not making any money. Start with promoting your product for free, be patient, and stay focused on one strategy!

I'm sure most of you have heard of "make money with google" products, I wouldn't even attempt getting into pay per visit right off the bat, it's way to risky as a new internet marketer.

Free Traffic

3. There are tons of ways you can promote the product that you have chosen! Here are some ideas that you can try.

EzineArticles - A very good place to start writing articles on your favorite subject, and you can include links to your product.

Yahoo! Answers - You can get a free account, and start answering questions for people, its easy. All you have to do is look up the question their asking and provide it to them. Make sure to answer 5-6 questions before sharing your affiliate link.

Google Groups - Get a free account there, another easy method. Join a group that is relative to the product you have chosen.

chosen. Again, make sure to participate in the groups discussion before putting your link out for your affiliate product.

Do Something

Thats right, do something! Alot of people fail because all they do is jump from one product launch to another, "Mr. Guru" is selling a new product so you get bombarded with all these ways to make money.

Stay focused on one strategy, like this <http://www.affiliateconquerer.com/coaching> one.

Give yourself some time. Your not gonna get rich over night. If your looking for some real intense training then this coaching <http://www.mavericktrainingclub.com> club will teach you everything you need to know about internet marketing (this is the only coaching club I suggest to family and friends).

So in conclusion, stay focused, pick your product wisely, and do one advertising strategy at a time till you make some money. -Brian

Why Affiliate Marketing Can 'Kill' Your Bills and Expenses Every Month

The internet is just not the greatest marketplace; it is also a goldmine if you know how to use it to your advantage. If you are a student or someone wanting to make money online fast then there is a lot of hope for you. Most people believe that you can't grow rich overnight, which is true but you surely can make fast cash. All you require is a PC and an internet connection.

Yes! We are talking about affiliate marketing and this is one market that has grown in leaps and bounds over the last 5-7 years.

So what is this business model we are talking about? It is more of relationship marketing where a company sells their products through an affiliate and the affiliate gets a certain amount of commission for the same. If you want to get into affiliate marketing then you need to have at least a website. This is important because as an affiliate you will need to place a link of the business whose affiliate program you have opted for.

Once you have a link on your website, people visiting your website will visit on these links and this might mean thousands of impressions every month. If the people visiting on the link to visit the company website buy the product or service then you will get a percentage of the sale or sometimes a flat rate. The important aspect is that the customer should buy the product but this is a win-win situation for you because you have nothing to lose.

Fabian Tan is a well-known Internet Marketing expert and the author of the popular 59-page Report:

"Murder Your Job: How To Build Cash Sucking Autopilot Businesses In 30 Days Or Less!"

Head over to http://www.MurderYourJob.com to get your FREE copy now!

Also, quickly download his FREE "Explosive Traffic System" report that shows you how to generate 10,000+ unique visitors per month at no cost! => http://www.ExplosiveTrafficSystem.com

Make Money Online - Affiliate Marketing

Perhaps one of the most common "make money online methods" is affiliate marketing. Over the years various

webmasters have been selling affiliate products to make money online.

What is affiliate marketing?

"Affiliate marketing" is the term used for the process of marketing products that belong to other companies which offer affiliate programs. Let me show you exactly how this system works:

1. A certain company creates a product and makes it available for promotion in their affiliate program.
2. An affiliate marketer finds the product trough their affiliate system and starts to promote it. (The product is usually promoted on a website, on a review page or even directly)
3. The affiliate marketer will get traffic to the page which contains the affiliate products to make sales.
4. When the affiliate marketer manages to make a sale, he will be awarded with a commission of the price.

The price of the commission will depend on the price of the products and the rates. Most companies will offer 60/40 or 50/50 revenue share, which means that you can make some good money if you promote a good product.

How to promote an affiliate product?

Promotion is the most difficult part in affiliate marketing. Everyone can find an affiliate product and promote it on a landing page but without traffic, you will not generate any sales.

Another important factor is the quality of the traffic. If you do some research you will find out that you can easily get some traffic but the question is: Is it targeted traffic?

Untargeted traffic will not generate any sales. Therefore, you need to bring targeted visitors to your site that are interested in your niche. One of the best ways to generate targeted traffic for free is by writing articles related to the product and submitting them to article directories. You can also work on getting back links by using blog commenting, social bookmarking and directory submission techniques. Apart from traffic, these methods are good for SEO and they will boost your website's ranking on search engines.

On the other hand if you have some money, you can advertise your site through PPC networks such as Google adwords.

Conclusion

As you should have noticed, the main thing here is targeted traffic. You can sell every product on earth if you bring targeted visitors to it, so I suggest that you start working on targeted traffic techniques immediately.

Kezia Johnson
Now that you've got a basic understanding of how to make money online- visit me at http://www.keziajohnson.info

Affiliate Marketing Tips - It's D-Day in Affiliate Marketing

Well, it's finally come down to this. In all my years of affiliate marketing, I never thought that I would see the day when affiliates really had to watch their backs. And I'm not talking about from competitors. I'm talking about from the actual products their promoting, both from merchants and from merchant marketplaces. It is getting ugly as sin out there. And while I can't go over all the problems, I will cover a few of the ones that I am aware of. Please tuck these in the back of your mind for safe keeping.

Let's start off with some shady merchants. These are the guys who really make my skin crawl. What some of them are doing now is redirecting prospects to a page that does NOT track your affiliate link. Or, what they'll do is get them onto their autoresponder and then in the follow-up series, send them links to their product that are on other domains. This way, you also don't get credit for the sale, even if you were tracked originally. I won't mention any names, but some big gurus are doing this. It's just sickening.

Another problem is with the marketplaces that some merchants use to host their products. Unfortunately, not all of them are up to par as far as tracking systems go. As a matter of fact, one giant affiliate marketplace is using a tracking system that is so antiquated that it is started to show signs of falling apart. The problem is that there is no incentive to fix the system because there is no real competition. As a result, affiliates are making sales but losing them because of tracking issues.

So, what do we do about this? Well, there are a number of things we can do as affiliates. One, is to make sure that when you promote an affiliate product, you give the customer incentive to write to you after the sale to confirm the purchase. This can be easily done by offering a bonus for buying from you. I do this with all my affiliate promotions and it works very well for me. The key is to make sure that you offer a bonus that compliments the product itself and makes the purchase a no brainer.

Affiliate marketing is going through a rough patch right now, but eventually things will work out.

They always do as long as you stay on your toes.

To YOUR Success,

Steven Wagenheim

Tired of being an affiliate failure? Want to turn yourself into an affiliate assassin like I am? Want to land in the top 20 of every affiliate promotion you tackle just like I do? Check out my site at http://www.stevewagenheim.com/affiliateassassin/index.html and start earning a solid income as an affiliate marketer.

Instant Cash Affiliate Programs - Making Fast Money Online

Instant Cash Affiliate Programs and Instant Commission Affiliate Programs have become a great way to make fast money online. With so many people looking for creative ways to make money and take care of those expected / unexpected cash needs, this is one of the more attractive ways to get your financial things done.

What better way than to have money paid to your PayPal account then through one or more reputable immediate payment affiliate programs? There aren't any that we've found.

Even better for yourself and your customers is your choosing to promote a product or service that you're passionate about. Choosing your product according to your passion will give you great credibility and motivate you toward providing great customer service. Ultimately, this is a win-win solution for both you and your customers.

What is meant by promoting a product you're passionate about? Simply put, if you love sports; specifically golf, then promoting golf instant payment program products would be best for you and your customers. They will sense your passion and sincerity and your credibility will soar. They'll look to you for answers to their needs and will look forward to every purchase opportunity you present. They may not always purchase but they will always remember how you've treated them.

By the way, getting involved with specialized markets is called niche marketing. Niche marketing is simply targeting a specific segment of the population to which you'll market a product or service. There are many instant cash affiliate programs and instant commission affiliate programs that will meet the needs of anyone's passion.

Whatever immediate payment affiliate programs you choose to promote will net you instant cash in your PayPal (must be business or premier verified) account. Making money fast online won't get any easier than this. Every sale of your instant cash affiliate product or instant commission affiliate product will send the cash payment directly and immediately into your PayPal account.

It's incredible. You actually have access to your money immediately. There's no faster way to make money online. And since you don't want any hype, there isn't any here. You can make as much money as you want; you just have to work for it while delivering excellent customer service. Remember, this is not going to make you rich but you will have cash readily available to you quickly and consistently.

So, what are you waiting for? Start Here to Increase Your Cash Flow and Earn $100 to $1000 <http://Emergency-Cash-Now.com> in as little as 24 Hours!

Affiliate Marketing Online Program - Stay on Top by Joining a Network

Joining an affiliate marketing online network is a fantastic way to help maximize your affiliate marketing returns while minimizing a lot of the research that most of affiliate marketers have to do in order to find quality affiliate programs that pay well and more importantly, have the potential to sell well.

Essentially, an affiliate marketing online program will compile many of the different affiliate marketing programs available on the Internet from all different categories and then offer its users metrics for discerning which programs they want to participate in. For instance, some of the better programs allow users to track how well certain affiliate programs are selling, how much money people are making and more importantly allow users to view this data that's been aggregated over time in such a way that they can monitor Internet trends to find when a product is selling hot and when it's time has come to be pulled from the market.

It is these metrics more than anything else that lends extra value to affiliate marketing online programs. If all of this raw data weren't enough to make up your mind about the value of these programs consider this; many affiliate marketers spent most of their time finding quality affiliate programs that they want to promote. Needless to say that the time spent researching programs cuts into the time spent setting up the affiliate sites and making money.

In fact some of the best affiliate marketers on the Internet have found ways to streamline this process to the point where they are up and running with new affiliates within minutes of finding them. Every minute that your affiliate connection is not up on the Internet is a minute that potential customers are buying from your competitors. Is it possible to be an affiliate marketer without enrolling in an online program? Definitely. But it is not something that most people would consider sustainable or wise.

If you want to discover a quick and effective way to make money online <http://theonlinemoneysecret.com> all you have to do is Go here <http://theonlinemoneysecret.com>

Learn Affiliate Marketing - Persistence is the Key

There is a definite catch 22 when it comes time for beginners to learn affiliate marketing. You can't really learn about these programs without taking action, and yet it is nearly impossible to successfully do affiliate marketing without learning about it first. Rather than becoming frustrated however it is important to realize that becoming a successful marketer is not in all or nothing proposition in the beginning. You don't have to be instantly successful in order to ensure your long-term success. In fact some of the most successful affiliate marketers have spoken publicly about how it took them months if not years to realize their full potential in this field of marketing.

Instead of thinking that you either have to learn or do, you should instead consider learning while doing. Understand that your first few months will be unsuccessful and concentrate your efforts on putting new techniques into practice while you are learning the in's and out's of affiliate marketing.

Affiliate marketing is fantastic in the fact that you do not have to be immediately successful for long term sustainable success. There is no pressure to make a name for yourself to help propel you into the future. You can utterly and completely fail within your first month, brush yourself off, reinvent your model and then an approach the business from a new informed perspective and succeed beyond your wildest dreams. It is the anonymous beauty of the Internet that allows new marketers to learn affiliate marketing at their own pace and adopt new techniques as they learn them without fear of ruining their "brand".

There are few other industries that allow this degree of complete flexibility so it is important that newcomers exploit it to its fullest potential. By completely embracing this rather than running from it new marketers can ensure their long-term success in the arena of online commerce.

If you want to discover a quick and effective way to make money online <http://theonlinemoneysecret.com> all you have to do is Go here <http://theonlinemoneysecret.com>

Affiliate Internet Marketing - Getting Past the First Month of Affiliate Sales

Affiliate internet marketing is the next big thing in online commerce that has been making waves on the Internet. It seems that nowadays everyone wants to be an affiliate marketer in order to earn themselves a little bit of extra side income without having to put in a lot of effort or time. Fortunately for the serious marketers these people quickly realize that in order to make a decent amount of money with affiliate into a marketing it is necessary to put in a good deal of time into the process in order to see returns that are meaningful. Sure you can make a dollar here and there without putting in any effort; but if you want to make hundreds or thousands of dollars you really need to treat affiliate marketing as its own type of business rather than a hobby.

The best way to learn about about affiliate programs is to sign up and do it. Don't jump into the water blind, of course, but really there's only so much you can learn from reading. A good compromise for people who are nervous about starting with no experience would be to spend a few days reading online guides about internet marketing, or even purchasing a well reviewed e-book about the subject and then jumping in feet first.

Managing your expectations in the first month or two is a critical step in ensuring your long-term success. Don't expect to make a lot of money right out of the gate. Your new at this, you need to spend time learning the process before you can expect great returns. The fantastic news is that once you understand the process it doesn't really change all that much overtime. Sure there are new trends that you must follow, products that once sold stop selling, and marketing programs that you relied upon for affiliates fail. While all of these circumstances can put a damper on your efforts it will not ruin it and once you become accustomed to rolling with the punches you'll find that this type of marketing is not only an easy way to make money it also be quite fun and even relaxing if you have the right mindset.

If you want to discover a quick and effective way to make money online <http://theonlinemoneysecret.com> all you have to do is Go here <http://theonlinemoneysecret.com>

Online Affiliate Marketing Programs - Find the Program That Perfectly Fits With You

When you look for online affiliate marketing programs you're more likely to find programs and services that you have to pay for rather than programs that you want to work for. This is the big issue when it comes to researching how to begin your new online business. Fear not however this is a process that everyone has had to go through when they want to start their online affiliate marketing business. In a way it's sort of like a rite of passage. Consider this the hazing that you must go through before entering into the fraternity of affiliate marketers.

The good news is that once you pass this initial test you will be able to very quickly make snap judgments about what online affiliate marketing programs are worth your time and which ones are just trying to sell you a service. This can be very confusing for beginners but once you have a little bit of experience under your belt you will quickly be able to separate them.

Here are a few quick pointers to help you get started. First of all make sure you fully understand what it is you are getting from any packages you sign up for. This especially holds true if you have to pay for them. If you're paying for an e-book or lesson about online affiliate marketing programs then make sure that the program covers everything you are interested in. If you're looking to join an affiliate network make sure that the network you are joining is up to date and constantly updated with new affiliates. By following these two basic tenets you should be able to quickly integrate yourself into the world of affiliate marketing.

If you want to discover a quick and effective way to make money online <http://theonlinemoneysecret.com> all you have to do is Go here <http://theonlinemoneysecret.com>

Ways to Make Money During the Recession

As the global economy heads into crisis mode more and more people are losing their jobs, but with no jobs being created we need to think up of alternative ways to make ends meat. In this article we are going to take a look at some alternative ways to make money during the recession and focus our attention on the internet.

We all have heard some sort of horror story about fraud online. Scam artists like to pray on the uneducated online user to exploit them for money. Yet in the midst of these scams there are many excellent online opportunities that can yield big profits. One of these ways to make money during the recession is called Internet Affiliate Marketing.

Internet Affiliate Marketing

Internet affiliate marketing is basically when you advertise a company's product for them and you earn a commission for every sale that goes through your advertisement first.

There are many ways you can advertise a product, these include:

Making advertising websites
E-mail marketing
Article marketing
Google AdSense - Pay Per Visit (PPC)
...and many more...

Internet affiliate marketing is without doubt the best and most profitable way to make money online. There are many people making up to $200,000 per year after only 2 years working as an internet marketer. Many people attempt to become affiliates but only the dedicated become that successful as it can up to 6 months of non-stop studying before you start making an income from it. Most people that search for ways to make money online are looking for a quick fix, but let me tell you now 'anything that promises you will make a lot of money very quickly is a scam!! '

With internet affiliate marketing it is all about patience and never giving up. If you stick to it you will become successful.

For More Information Visit Wealthy Affiliate Review <http://www.wealthyaffiliate-reviewer.com>

How to Make a Good Living Online

When it comes to learning how to make a good living online, most people won't know where to start from. We hear in forums and other forms of contact with others online that MOST get rich quick products online are complete and utter scams, set up by people who are quite content to take money off people that are obviously in some form of money trouble, otherwise they wouldn't be resorting to these type of money making opportunities.

For the person with little or no knowledge of how the internet works it will be very hard to make a good living online for a number of years as there is so much to learn. But for the more determined person willing to spend time, effort and a little cash is is certainly possible to make money online and it is even possible to make enough money to be able to quit your day job and live off the cash you earn on-line.

Affiliate marketing is one of the more common ways to make a good living online

What is affiliate marketing?

Affiliate marketing is when you promote (market) some other persons product. For every sale you get for that person you will get a portion of the sale. In some cases it can be as high as 75% of the sale if you are selling eBooks or such products. The percentage for these products is so high as it cost the merchant (owner of the product) nothing to sell as it is simply a wire transfer

There are potentially very big earning to be made from affiliate marketing online but there are so many people doing it and not all last very long.

Only the truly determined affiliate marketers will be able to make a living out it it but it is definitely possible and certainly is not rocket science.

For More Information Visit Wealthy Affiliate Review <http://www.wealthyaffiliate-reviewer.com>

Affiliate Marketing Business Success in 3 Steps

Going into business as an affiliate marketer online can be a very rewarding experience, however there are some vital steps you'll need to take.

One of the first things you'll need to do is get yourself some tools to get your affiliate marketing business operational. These tools are a domain name, Web hosting and a website. With these tools you will be able to create unique landing pages that will house the programs and products you wish to promote.

The second thing you'll want to start doing right away is building a list of prospects that you can market to on an ongoing basis. The purpose for the list is to capitalize on all of the visitors who come to your site but don't buy anything. If there is no auxiliary system in place for contacting those leads, than you would essentially be leaving money on the table.

The third and last step you'll will continually work at is mastering the art of driving massive targeted visitors to your site on a continual basis. Without visitors coming to your site, your chances for success are virtually nonexistent. Setting up a daily routine for getting traffic to your website is vital to the lifeblood of your business.

These three steps when applied can help you to become a successful affiliate and developing a long term affiliate marketing business online. There are a variety of methods you can use to promote affiliate products and programs for ongoing profit. As is the case with most businesses there are tricks to the trade that you can leverage for faster profits.

If you would like to get more details concerning the tricks of the trade in the affiliate marketing business <http://www.massiveautopilotincome.com> , you're invited to download 4 Free affiliate marketing reports that will show you exactly how to make money online with your own affiliate marketing business <http://www.massiveautopilotincome.com> .

Getting Started in the Affiliate Marketing Business

The affiliate marketing business is growing very fast and it's becoming a great source for alternate income. To get started successfully with affiliate marketing getting the right information is crucial.

There are lots of affiliate programs available for someone to participate in, but not all are created equal.

Finding a good affiliate program is vital to your success online. There are dozens of products that you can promote as an affiliate marketer, but it is important to know how to pick the ones that will yield the greatest return on investment of time and resources.

As an affiliate marketer it is important to understand the simple concept of pre-selling your prospects to the merchants sales page. All too often many affiliates make the mistake of trying to sell. It can be confusing when you're first starting out.

When promoting affiliate marketing programs or products it's vital to understand how to leverage the work of the product or program owner so as to take the weight off of your own efforts.

Starting out with your affiliate marketing business will require you to be organized. You will obtain tons of links to promote the various affiliate products and programs you choose. The last thing you want to do is kill time searching through a stack of papers to find a link to a particular program you wish to promote.

Time is your most valuable asset as an affiliate marketer and how you leverage it will determine your ultimate success. There are lots of resources that are available to assist you with managing your time effectively, but you will need to assess each one individually in order to determine it's value to your business.

The affiliate marketing business <http://www.massiveautopilotincome.com> can be a very rewarding one provided you have the knowledge and basic understanding of how to make it work for you. If you would like to get information that will show you how to get started fast with affiliate marketing download 4 free reports that will give you the details you need for getting started in the affiliate marketing business <http://www.massiveautopilotincome.com> .

How to Fight the Downward Recession Graph by Working Online

The global economy is now in recession and jobs are few and far between at the moment, but what if I was to tell you that internet spending was up by 19% in the month of January 2009, compared to the month of January 2008... FACT!

Internet spending is expected to rise by 10.7% annually and will hit a massive $600 billion annual spend by the year 2011. The United States is currently the front runner in internet spending, although China is expected to overtake the U.S. by the year 2010.

With these massive amounts of cash being spent online it opens many doors to would-be internet entrepreneurs. I am going to take a look at one to fight the downward recession graph by working online.

Internet Affiliate Marketing

Internet affiliate marketing is when you advertise a company's product for them and receive commission for every sale they get that goes through your affiliate link first. There are many forms of advertising that affiliates use, both paid and free. These include article marketing, website creation, PPC and many more.

You can be an affiliate for pretty much any product that is available online from tiles to gambling website memberships and you can get anywhere from 1% commission per sale right up to 75% commission per sale.

There is an initial period of study to be done before you can successfully start making sales on a regular basis. This period of study can take anywhere from 1 week to 6 months depending on the initiative, dedication and previous computer skills of the person starting the course. Many people that become successful as internet affiliate marketers do so with no prior computer or internet experience.

After you have completed the study course, potential earnings can be from $20,000 - $100,000 in year 1. The global recession graph may be on a downward slope but you can do more than just keep your head above water by choosing to work online

For More Information Visit Wealthy Affiliate Review <http://www.wealthyaffiliate-reviewer.com>

How to Make Extra Money Once You've Retired

Everyone who works a job is going to retire someday. And many of you who have retired will be looking to make some extra money once you have. You could get a paper route, or mow lawns or work in a hardware store, but I think there's a better way.

The fact you're even reading this shows you're online, so why don't we stay here? If someone were to ask me how to make extra money once you've retired I would definitely choose affiliate marketing as my answer.

For those who don't know, affiliate marketing is when you sell someone elses' products online for a commission. It isn't like regular cold calling type selling though. There are very specific strategies you will use to gain prospective customers. It can be a little complicated sometimes, but make no mistake about it, affiliate marketing is a great way to make extra money once you've retired. All you really need is an internet connection, a computer, and a good online education.

The value of a good education is priceless, and that certainly goes for your affiliate marketing business. Why bother doing it at all if you aren't going to do it right? When you arm yourself with the knowledge it takes to succeed, everything will be that much easier.

The best place that I've found to learn the ins and outs of affiliate marketing has to be Wealthy Affiliate. They are an online community full of tutorials and forums and everything you'll ever need to succeed online. If you're going to learn how to do it, might as well learn from the best, right?

It is very possible to make over six figures with affiliate marketing if you know what you're doing. As a retiree, you may not need or want that much, but it's out there if you do. All you have to do is learn how to do it.

If you're retired, and really want to make some extra money <http://reviewthewealthyaffiliate.blogspot.com> with affiliate marketing...learn how to do it right. Go look here right now for everything you'll ever need: Wealthy Affiliate Review <http://reviewthewealthyaffiliate.blogspot.com>

Money Making Machine - With Affiliate Marketing, Even a Baby Can Count in Millions

Waiting eagerly for your pension or gratuity sounds like a great idea to me; however, of what use is it to get that money when you are too weak to enjoy life? This is why majority have chosen to grab it young. Are you looking for a safe and reliable system developed and proven to generate hundreds of dollars from home each day? Do you wish to show your family the love they deserve? Are you interested in doing something that you love? Would you like to stop messing up your credit history because of not paying your bills on time? Have you always wanted a job that will offer you the opportunity to work at your own pace? Do you want to start making the money you deserve right from the comfort of your home? If yes; then, make a resolution to turn around your life for good.

Maybe, you still doubt the authenticity of what people says each time they come up with the ideas on how people are making millions online each year through affiliate marketing. Well it is not your fault, as there are lots of people out there that think the same way. However, most people have switched from their stumbling blocks into stepping stones; because, they decided to make sacrifices that involved money, decision making, determination and discipline. Make this an opportunity to join millions of people in America who are already making lots of money online even while economy gets worst. With the right tools, you can make a living through affiliate marketing business online, and since the internet never sleeps, programs has been developed to help you get cash deposits into your account even while you are sleeping.

Someone whose this is his/her first time to hear about affiliate marketing may come up with the two questions listed below,

Question #1
What the heck does he mean by affiliate marketing?

Answer

Putting it short, affiliate marketing is the combination of software and ideas that individuals use to track money online from any part of the world.

Question #2

Who is qualified to be an affiliate marketer?

Answer

A: Anyone that can read as well as type on a computer

B: Anyone that loves making money

C: Anyone that wish to say no to isolation

the good news is that you do not need to go to college like majority did, you also do not need to have any experience with software, programming, networking, or desktop publishing to make money online using the right systems. If you truly know how to check your email and surf the web; then, the sky is your limit. With affiliate marketing program, you no longer need to pick up a call or talk to a customer, all you need is to explore a little of your potential, and then sit back and watch the cash as it flows into your bank account.

Finally, to achieve success in any thing, you need to be determined as well as goal oriented, and making money online through affiliate marketing is not an exception. There is no need to spend time again figuring out what works, there is also no need to go through search engines just to find a reliable way of making money; because, all these has already been done for you. You do not need to worry again about getting fired or laid off, and you do not have to be afraid to open your mail box due to fear of incoming bills, having your alarm clock wake you up when you are about to enjoy your sleep will be a thing of the past.

Want to stay at home and make more money than your boss? Now you can find everything you have always wanted in just one place, but first, you have to act fast because this offer will not last forever. To check it out, visit: http://www.Smartmillionares.Com/

Are You Curious About What is the Easiest Affiliate Marketing Method?

That is an interesting and difficult question to say the least. It is my opinion that there is no easiest affiliate marketing method. All affiliate marketing takes research, education, knowledge, wisdom, trial and error and hard work.

Some people say that using pay-per-visit is the easiest affiliate marketing method. In a sense pay-per-visit is fairly easy to set up. However, pay-per-visit can be very expensive, and there is also a very strong learning curve in pay-per-visit.

In addition, pay-per-visit using an affiliate landing page can be very expensive because it is naturally more expensive to use an affiliate landing page rather than your own. In a way, this keeps affiliate marketers from saturating too much of the pay per visit market.

I have actually lost quite a bit of money using this method before I actually learned about keyword research and how to set up proper campaigns. Even after this learning, pay per visit can still add up and is actually still quite expensive if your product does not convert well. Putting up banner ads and AdSense on your already created blog or website is quite easy to do. I have not had the greatest conversions using this method. You need A LOT of traffic to your blog or website to truly monetize in this area.

I think one of the best, and fairly easy ways to do affiliate marketing is to set up blogs for each niche market that you want to focus on. You can set up Blogger.com blogs and talk about your subject, using keywords as anchor text to your affiliate program. I think this is one of the easiest affiliate marketing methods, and one of the most affordable as well!

Michelle Tukachinsky is a successful internet and affiliate marketer. You can learn more about her by visiting her blog at http://www.money-online.tv

Recession Trends - Make Money Online During This Recession

Yet another global recession is upon us. Recession trends have stayed true to themselves once again. Consumer spending is at a decade low and not only are people losing their job, but no jobs are being created. With all this doom and gloom on the economic front it may surprise you to learn that internet spending went up by 19% in the last 12 months and it is expected to continue to rise by a further 10.7% per year over the next 4 years. This opens the door of opportunity for many would-be internet entrepreneurs to make, not only a full time living working online, but to make upwards of a 6 figure salary. Today we are going to take a look at one of the best ways to make money online, even with current recession trends.

Internet Affiliate Marketing

Internet affiliate marketing is when you advertise a company's product for them and get a commission for every sale you get for the company through your advertisement. You can be an affiliate for literally any product that is sold online, from products on Amazon to information eBooks on how to build muscle, lose weight, cure impotence, get the girl or even how to be a better person (yes these products exist and what is more amazing is they actually sell!!!). You can advertise such products by both free and paid methods including article marketing, PPC, SEO, email marketing, web development and many more different ways.

The vast majority of affiliate marketing programs are free to join and you can earn any where from 1% commission right up to 75% commission for any sales you get through your ads. For any sales you make you will either get paid by check (cheque), PayPal, or directly into your bank account.

Internet affiliate marketing needs some studying to get the techniques down to a tee, but once you have these figured out the possibilities are endless.

What is the potential salary for an affiliate marketer?

There are many marketers that have only started working as an affiliate in the last 2-3 years and are now on $200,000 annual salaries. This type of salary is not uncommon at all but it just takes a lot of work and dedication to reach this level of success. Many marketers will hit the $30,000 after one year as an affiliate but since internet spending is up this year and is expected to rise further, even with recession trends, there could be a possibility for much greater profits.

For More Information Visit Wealthy Affiliate Review <http://www.wealthyaffiliate-reviewer.com>

Some Points to Boost Your Affiliate Marketing Business

Are you new to affiliate marketing business? Do you want to do good even if you just started doing it? Are you an affiliate marketer for quite some time now and looking for some helpful tips to even make your business better and be able to rake in more cash? Without a doubt you want to check on the following points to help you with your business.

To begin with, you must choose companies with a long list of customer. Being able to do that means that you are expanding your customer base. It is a fact that if you have a large customer base, chances of making sales is also big.

Another thing that can be done is to create promotional ads for your company and those companies you are affiliated with. You might want to utilize all kinds of advertising medium to promote your business. You can create an advertising video or article that covers your company and your partners company. How are you going to pay for the costs it may incur? You may want to share it with the companies you are affiliated with. It will do good for the both of your business and can save some cash.

Finally, you can be an affiliate for as many companies as you want. Having so many companies you are affiliated with means more customers you can reach. Just some words of caution though, you need to conduct background check for each company you wanted to be an affiliate of. You must make sure that all these companies are reputable.

Fernand Dizon writes on a variety of subjects. To learn more about affiliate marketing, please visit his blog site <http://www.super-affiliate-tools.com>

Recession Cycle - Can We Make Money Through the Recession?

The ominous recession cycle has come back around again, but with this recession also comes opportunity. Internet spending has increased by 19% over the last 12 months and is set to increase by 10.7% annually for the next 4 years. This opens many doors of opportunity to both businesses and individuals alike looking to sell their products or information online. Today we are going to take a look at one of the most popular ways a person can make money online.

Internet Affiliate Marketing

Internet affiliate marketing has been around since 1994 but has only very become popular in the last 5 years as more and more advanced education courses come on the market. Internet affiliate marketing is when you advertise a product or service for a company and get commission for every sale you get that goes through your advertisement first.

There are many different ways you can advertise a product for a company, both free and paid. These include article marketing, website development, SEO techniques, PPC, email marketing and many more.

You can literally be an affiliate for almost any product on the market and nearly all affiliate marketing programs are free to join. You can earn anywhere from 1% commissions up to 75% commissions for every sale you get through your advertisement and you can get paid by check (cheque) or directly in your PayPal account depending on the affiliate program.

What are the potential earnings for internet marketing during this recession cycle?

Potential earnings for affiliate marketing can reach up to $60,000 in year 1. $100,000 in year 2 and only onwards and upwards from there as you gather new skills to target more expensive products with larger commissions. One of the best aspects of affiliate marketing is that it allows you to be your own boss, to work you own hours as you choose and to work from the comfort of your own home.

With an expected $600 billion dollars projected annual internet spend by the year 2011, there is massive potential for affiliate marketers to become successful, even in this current recession cycle.

For More Information Visit Wealthy Affiliate Review <http://www.wealthyaffiliate-reviewer.com>

Success at Affiliate Marketing - Is it Attainable?

If you are reading this in hopes of learning the magic formula of success at Affiliate marketing, I've got news for you that I will share at the end of this article. No article, or eBook, or video, or tutorial, can teach you all you'll need to know of how to have success in this competitive, highly skilled, and complicated profession. Expecting to learn how to have success with affiliate marketing by reading an article, is as likely as learning how to become a doctor by reading an article. In today's economy, with so many people losing their jobs and turning to affiliate marketing as an income option, the affiliate marketing industry is becoming more and more competitive. We are entering a new era in this industry, where only the best will survive. So if you want to know how to have success with affiliate marketing, it is by thoroughly understanding how affiliate marketing works. You must get well educated in every aspect of the inner workings of Internet and affiliate marketing. Anything short of becoming a well-trained, educated professional will ultimately mean the difference between success and failure.

To learn how to have success with affiliate marketing, it is becoming more and more important to join Internet Marketing University, which will be discussed further in a moment. Sure, there are tons of programs, courses, tutorial, and eBooks out there that claim they can teach you what you need to know, but do they really? Most of these programs are outdated, or merely a sales pitch for other products. Many of them do contain some good concepts and ideas, but they don't give you the basics of Internet marketing, so you end up having more questions than answers. Babies don't learn to run before they learn to walk.

When you first enter the members' area of Wealthy Affiliate University, you will be amazed at how much information there is, how many tools there are. You will wonder how you will ever figure it all out. You will wonder where to start. Then you will notice that there is an 8-week plan that lays out everything you need to do in a chronological, methodical, useful, order. You will be given lessons, tutorials, videos and tasks to accomplish. As you go through your 8 week plan you will become proficient at every aspect of affiliate and Internet marketing. You will be given tools of the trade to learn and use, such as the website builder, keyword search tool, competition spy tool, and more. You will learn how to choose a good product and niche to market, and will do so. You will learn how to specialize, and will master one type of marketing, while you learn all. You will put together a marketing campaign that will rival the top marketers in skill and quality, and you will be coached, advised and supported along the way. You will become a professional in every sense of the word, and you will learn how to truly earn thousands of dollars per day in this industry.

People who try to learn how to have success with affiliate marketing on their own usually only find frustration, large credit card bills (due to buying a bunch of stuff that they didn't need or use), and failure. And with each day that passes, the affiliate marketing industry becomes a more competitive, tougher place to earn a living. Without the best affiliate training you can get, such as that at Wealthy Affiliate University, you will not achieve your desired dreams of success at affiliate marketing. That is a cold, hard truth.

Get $1000 worth of FREE business eBooks and software at http://www.wealthy-affiliate-university-bonus.info

Affiliate Mistakes - How to Avoid Them?

Affiliate marketing is a lucrative way to earn online and more and more people are being attracted to this business. Affiliate programs are free to join, easy to set up and can be started free of cost. It provides an opportunity to earn money even for the new internet entrepreneur. There are hundreds of affiliate programs available online. To be successful in affiliate marketing business, you have to avoid certain mistakes and pitfalls, otherwise these may cost you a large part of your profits. The following are the different mistakes which must be avoided:

1. Choosing the wrong affiliate program - The first mistake is to choose the wrong affiliate program. There are thousands of affiliate programs available online. But choosing the right affiliate program is difficult. Before joining an affiliate program, you must do thorough research about it. Do not just jump for a program only because it offers a high commission. The product selected should appeal to you and it should be of high quality. The product should have a high demand and it should be relevant to the topic of your website. For example, if you run a website on pet care and try to promote some internet marketing E books from your site, your efforts will be wasted.
2. Joining a large number of affiliate programs - The second mistake is to join a large number of affiliate programs at the same time. Joining an affiliate program is free and easy. There is a tendency among newbie affiliate marketers to join a large number of programs at the same time hoping to earn money from all of them. But promoting different products at the same time is difficult. The best thing for an affiliate marketer is to start with only one program (preferably which offers a high commission) and put all his efforts into promoting that one. After you become successful with your first program and gain some knowledge about different internet marketing techniques, you can try promoting other programs.
3. Not using the product yourself - Before promoting any product, you should buy and use the same yourself. In that way, you can gain knowledge about the advantages and disadvantages of using that product and can convince your customers about the same.

Try to avoid these common mistakes and you will be successful in your affiliate marketing business.

Rahul Arora has been a Web Developer for the last 4 years and is an expert in onpage SEO and creating web apps. You could always follow his blog at http://blog.dir.vc/

Successful Affiliate Marketing Businesses

A popular Internet marketing strategy is to start an affiliate marketing venture, which removes some of the risk from your end, although you will need to take care and run this as you would any other business. If this will be your sole source of income, you will have to be especially heedful of how you run this business, wanting to give it your all. There are a number of Internet marketing strategies, however, that you can use to get your business going and make it strong and successful.

The most important part of any Internet marketing strategies is to know what is in demand. In affiliate marketing, you will probably be trying to market a number of different products and you will absolutely need to know what the demand for these products is like. Trendy products are generally something that you will want to avoid, as the best type of products to market are the ones that people will always want. This is how you will build a long-term business that will always be working for you.

Indeed, along these same lines, you will want to offer a variety of products. The more that you can offer your customers, the more reasons they will have to return. If you try to affiliate market with a small selection, someone will eventually come along that will offer better products at a better price than you do. If, therefore, you offer more, you give consumers a reason to keep visiting you.

Another helpful Internet marketing strategy is to establish how you are different from all of the competitors. If you can point out what makes you different from all of the other businesses out there without painting them in a negative light, you can entice people to shop with you. If you use tact and never make negative remarks about the competition, you will show that you are a classy retailer and that you can give the customer everything they might want.

Two things that you should always do are to insure your business and always tell the truth to your customers. Insuring your business can be important because in case something goes wrong and one of your products ends up being damaged, you will want to be sure that you are protected against any damages that may result. Telling the truth is also important because, while you will do your best to assure efficient service to your customers, sometimes glitches do happen. It is best to simply be upfront with your customers about this, it will earn their respect much more than a lie ever would.

The best of the Internet marketing strategies, however, all revolve around keeping the customer happy. By doing this, you will ensure repeat customers and this is something that any successful business needs. Affiliate marketing can be very profitable, for it removes the typical risks of starting an online business. It, however, will need all of the attention that a self-run business needs. With a little hard work and dedication, however, you can make this work for you!

Kimberlyn Lebsock has been an entrepreneur for more than 20 years. She has started, owned, and operated several multimillion dollar businesses. She has also spent thousands of dollars on her Internet Marketing education and has found major success marketing with Internet platform opportunities that are already in place and they work. http://www.groundfloor.wordpress.com Her primary focus is to show millions of people how they also can achieve success with a business online. Kimberlyn's web site offers an incredible opportunity to people who want to create passive income with an online venture or want to create massive income with a combination of online and offline strategies. With Kimberlyn's abilities to share strategies and guide her team to success is where she has been most successful. Coaching teams of people through product knowledge for sales and territory development, her teams learn how to skyrocket their income using an existing online platform.

Kimberlyn is a mentor and a coach by nature, using existing systems that work. She has developed currently a large team nationally and will be expanding internationally soon. Kimberlyn assists people by taking their abilities to the next level, and be on the road to success, as quickly, effortlessly, and cost effectively as possible. She is located in beautiful Southern California, and through her website, is able to serve new and seasoned entrepreneurs nationwide.

INDEX*

59-page Report, popular 117-18, 152, 155

A
Adapp Solutions 53, 68-9, 72, 74
ads 17, 37-8, 45, 64-5, 96, 143, 176
  classified 143-4
AdSense ads 64-5
advertise 15, 23, 28, 80, 97, 113, 118, 143, 157, 166, 171, 176, 178-9
advertisements 13-14, 113, 121, 147-8, 166, 176, 179
  selling 28
advertisers 22, 44-5, 53, 72, 142, 147
advertiser's website 22
advertising 13, 15, 22, 28, 61, 68, 72, 76, 94, 97, 117, 121, 127, 132, 134, 146-7 [2]
advice 1, 5, 30, 34, 41-2, 95, 98, 133
affiliate advertisements 36
affiliate assassin 158
Affiliate Avalanche 144
affiliate business uses 147
affiliate businesses 10, 59, 124, 146-7
affiliate cloaker 106
affiliate commissions 7, 33, 46, 88, 117-18
affiliate companies 37, 124
affiliate connection 161
affiliate contests 118
affiliate failure 158
affiliate Fuel 129
Affiliate Funnel System 9, 111-12
Affiliate Funnel System Review 9, 111
Affiliate Funnel System Work 112
affiliate identification 66
affiliate income 47
affiliate internet marketing 7, 10, 49, 163
affiliate internet marketing goals 51
affiliate internet marketing successes 49
affiliate links 7-9, 25, 37-8, 64-6, 75, 78, 105-6, 116, 128, 153, 158, 171
  cloak 66
  personal 24
  special 145
  unique 13
affiliate login ID, unique 146
affiliate management companies 146
affiliate management program 42
affiliate managers 146
affiliate market 183
affiliate marketer 34-5, 42, 47-9, 53-5, 60, 63, 74, 76, 87, 130-1, 156, 159-61, 163-4, 169-70, 174-5, 177 [8]

affiliate marketer manages 156
affiliate marketer online 168
affiliate marketing 6-11, 23-6, 33-6, 47-9, 53-9, 71-4, 88-9, 95-6, 112-13, 119-21, 128-31, 134, 154-8, 162-3, 172-5, 178-81 [21]
  drive 122
  love 42
  what is 95
affiliate marketing business 7, 11, 24, 61-2, 121-3, 142, 168-70, 172, 177, 182
affiliate marketing business online 173
  long term 168
Affiliate Marketing Business Success 11, 168
Affiliate Marketing Businesses 11, 183
affiliate marketing companies 37
affiliate marketing download 170
affiliate marketing efforts 73
Affiliate Marketing Fast 8, 88
affiliate marketing income 33
affiliate marketing industry 180-1
affiliate marketing methods 175
Affiliate Marketing Mindset 135
Affiliate Marketing Newbies 9, 129
affiliate marketing online 113, 167
affiliate marketing online program 7, 10, 53-4, 160-1
Affiliate Marketing Part 109
affiliate marketing plugin 42
affiliate marketing programs 7, 9, 48, 56, 120-1, 147, 151, 161, 169, 174, 176, 179
  casino 115
affiliate marketing review 89
Affiliate Marketing Secrets 9, 117
affiliate marketing site 63
affiliate marketing software 72
Affiliate Marketing Strategies 8, 79, 153
Affiliate Marketing Tips 7, 9-10, 78, 116, 151, 157
affiliate marketing topics 148
affiliate marketing venture 183
Affiliate Marketing Website 7, 72
affiliate marketing.You 142
affiliate merchant 123-4
affiliate merchant's website 93
Affiliate Mistakes 11, 181
affiliate net-works 53, 72
affiliate networks 69, 71-2, 123-4, 138-9, 146, 165
  largest 78
affiliate offerings 37
affiliate plan 52
affiliate pro-gram 24, 83, 100
affiliate products 37-8, 105, 116, 124, 148, 154, 156, 158, 168-9
  best 130

competing 144
income marketing 15
instant cash 160
instant commission 160
selling 156
affiliate products online 34
affiliate programs 6, 8-10, 13-15, 24, 65-6, 71-2, 77, 93-4, 101-2, 107, 119-20, 144-6, 151, 155-6, 169, 181-2 [9]
best free 129
cheap advertising space 120
eBay's 80
excellent 77
high-paying 64
large number of 182
minority of 26
multi-tier 102
payment 159-60
quality 101-2, 161
ready-made 107
reliable 13
residual income 6, 18-19
right 103, 182
selling 120
two-tier 51, 66
web 66
affiliate promotions 118, 158
Affiliate Referrals 7, 51, 66
affiliate revenue 1, 5, 80
Affiliate Revenue strategies, best 5
affiliate sales 10, 77, 115, 119, 125, 128-9, 163
affiliate seller 104
affiliate sign-up 107
affiliate sites 27, 114, 161
competing 128
affiliate software 69, 74
Affiliate Strategy 79-80
affiliate system 156
complete super 94
two-tiered 69
affiliate thief, common 106
affiliate tools 28
affiliate training personnel 71
affiliate website 101, 144
affiliated product 106
affiliated programs 17
AffiliateLinks.ht ml 66
AffiliateMarketing 96
affiliatemarketingtips 98
affiliates 6, 20, 25-6, 33-5, 57-8, 66-9, 95, 101, 107-8, 113-14, 117-20, 132-3, 146, 155, 157-8, 175-9 [22]

multiple 123
new 6, 90, 120-1, 161, 165
paying 138
right 130
super 94
top 89
affiliates marketing 129
affiliates programs online 123
affiliation 3, 149
answer 45, 48, 50, 56, 59-60, 96, 99-100, 103-4, 110, 133, 153, 159, 172, 174, 180
article directories 22, 36, 38, 41, 83, 157
article marketing 21-2, 36, 38, 41, 83, 118, 166, 171, 176, 179
Article Marketing Traffic 83
audience 15-16, 72-3
automate 132-3
Automated Income Online 9
autopilot 9, 77, 131-2
autoresponder 133
avenue 87, 100-1

B
backlinks 39, 41
banners 15, 27-8, 33, 113, 116-17, 130
basics 7, 69, 74, 180
be-comes 45, 47
beginners 14, 16, 162, 164
Beginners to Affiliate Marketing 54
beliefs 7, 46-7, 59
believing 86-7, 144
bestproductsreviews.info/newbieworkbook 90
bills 10, 37, 62, 77, 86-7, 91, 154, 173
blog hosting website, free 54
blog page 54
Blogger.com 36-7, 54
blogging 14, 36
blogs 13, 15, 31, 36, 38-9, 41, 53-4, 65, 67, 70, 73-4, 76, 80, 85, 116, 175 [5]
high-trafficked 117
board 82
Bob 144-5
Body Language Expert 47, 49, 51, 56, 60
bonus 128-9, 133, 140, 158
great 129
book 3, 5, 55-7, 145
boxes 36
boxes of cookies 50
Build Cash Sucking Autopilot Businesses 117-18, 152, 155
building 7, 62, 64, 72, 76-8, 84, 130-1, 133-4, 168
bum marketing 36, 38

business 26, 29-30, 41-2, 53-4, 60-2, 64, 69-70, 72-3, 97-9, 126-7, 132, 140-2, 148-9, 168, 177-8, 183-4 [17]
based 82
cleaning 145
large 133
legitimate 135
long-term 183
profitable 87
self-run 184
solid 41, 148
business consultant 144
business elements 127
business entities 145
business environment, changing 145
business expert 92
business interests 126
business model 88, 155
right 36
business online 41, 184
business opportunity customers 107
business plan 93
business practices 122
business world 134

C

camera, buy x model digital 39
campaigns 20, 25, 38, 90, 105, 132, 175
Canada 145
career 121-2
Carson 148-9
cash 30, 43, 91, 160, 167, 174, 177-8
Casino affiliate marketing 114
Casino Affiliate Marketing 9, 114
casino affiliate marketing website 115
chairs 46
change 8, 21, 70, 86-7, 92, 99-100, 136, 163
Chitika 16-17
Choose Affiliate Programs 10, 151
christiankostyo@gmail.com 82
cities 143
clients 50, 104, 147
cloak 8, 105-6
college fees 111
com/affiliate-marketing-review.html 89
comers 148
Commission Junction 74, 80, 123, 153
commission tracking link, associated 106
commissions 9, 13-14, 18, 30-1, 45, 60, 68-9, 77-8, 101-3, 105, 130-1, 138-9, 155-6, 171-2, 176, 179 [12]
high 182

commitment 32, 52, 126-7
companies 3, 37, 40, 48, 53, 71, 74, 82, 95, 101, 134, 142, 146, 155-6, 176-9
company's website 15, 95
compensation plans 147
Complete Money Making Site Setup 116
computer 29, 36, 44, 57, 81, 92, 95-6, 99, 172, 174
cons 17, 67, 106
consumers 75, 123-4, 183
contact 43, 82, 104, 129, 143, 166
content 6, 45, 65, 67, 72-3, 75, 93, 108, 115, 118, 120, 125, 167
content websites/blogs 22
control 50-1, 86, 95, 122, 135
conversion rate 104-5, 125
conversions 104-5
cookies 50
Copyright 2009-Vincent Harris-All Rights Reserved 47, 49, 51, 56
cost 18, 27, 33, 44, 70, 75, 80, 85, 88, 117, 119, 123, 147, 149, 152, 181-2 [4]
couple 29, 36, 110-11, 130, 152
CPA 80, 88-9, 147
CPC 147
CPM methods 147
credibility 37, 159
customer service 159
  excellent 160
customers 14, 20, 29-30, 44, 61-2, 64, 72, 77, 84, 101, 107-8, 115, 129, 159, 177-8, 182-4 [5]
  affiliate's 54
  potential 70, 128, 161
  target 122, 129

D

D-Day in Affiliate Marketing 10, 157
David Cooper's Affiliate Marketing 144
decision 93, 95, 99, 101-4, 173
designations 3
digital products 48-9, 55, 57-8, 60, 101, 138
dime 98
directories online, trafficked 118
discovery 47, 49, 51, 56
display 145-7
divorce 55
dollars 13, 22, 27, 31, 91, 113, 119, 142-3, 163, 173, 179, 181, 184
domain 36-7, 76, 134, 158
domain name 38, 75, 81-2, 107, 114, 125, 168
Domains International 8
donnieseasymoney.com 148
download 20, 88, 117-18, 152, 155, 168
dreams 30, 32, 34, 87, 96-7, 146, 162, 181

affiliate's 89

E
e-mail 25-6, 43, 64, 66
Earn Money 7, 56
earning 14, 46, 51, 57, 66, 68, 135, 167
based business 78
home-based business 116
potential 171, 179
Easy Ways to Make Money 6, 21
ebooks 27, 48, 55, 57, 123
eBooks 35, 180
economy 19, 48, 81-2, 95, 99, 136, 173, 180
eighty 147
energy conservation 134-5
Excellent affiliate marketing tools 149
experience 22, 28, 50, 54, 56, 90, 98-9, 104, 121, 126-7, 163-4, 168, 174
expert 5, 73, 76, 183
expert internet marketer 79
Explosive Traffic System report 117-18, 152, 155
Extraordinary Amount of Money 9
Extraordinary Amount of Money Online 113
ezines 26-7, 117

F
failure 20, 70, 180-1
fantasy 57
Fast Money Maker 6
Favorite Ways Make Money 26
features, best 149
fight 11, 170
Finally 6, 21, 23, 77, 115, 174, 178
firms 13-14
First Affiliate Marketing Check 6, 29
First Month of Affiliate Sales 10, 163
Fitzgeraldsuccess.com 140-1
focus 31-2, 55, 108, 111, 121, 123, 142, 152, 165, 175
formed goal 49-50
forum marketing 40, 84, 116
forums 13, 34-5, 40-1, 55, 62-3, 115-16, 166, 172
foundation 22, 99, 132
fraction 64
frauds 147
Free affiliate marketing reports 168
FREE business eBooks 35, 96, 181
FREE copy 117-18, 152, 155
Free Internet Marketing Strategy 10, 152
fun 34, 62, 64, 95, 106, 164

G

gambling website memberships 171
gas masks 48
GDI 81-2
GDI members 82
generalization 46, 58-9
get Rich Quick websites 110
Getting Insane Amounts of Traffic 8, 83
Gifting Type Programs 27
gifts 7, 27-8, 48-9, 55
gling work 59
Global Domains International 81-2
Global Domains International Opportunity 82
goals 7, 31-2, 49-52, 58, 71, 109, 146, 148, 150-1, 174
golf 109, 153, 159
gonna 136-7, 154
gonna work 136
Google 20, 27, 29, 36, 64-5, 94, 97, 101, 125, 143-4
groups 47, 85, 150, 153
guarantee 42, 104, 108, 140
guide 16, 69, 89-90, 153, 185

H

Harris, Vincent 47, 49, 51, 56, 58-60
head 47, 57, 87, 117-18, 152, 155, 171
Hints 1, 5
hobbies 6, 34-5, 140, 153, 163
home 7, 9, 19, 23-4, 31, 34, 50, 53-4, 71, 78, 81-2, 95, 113, 123-5, 134-6, 173-4 [7]
home business model 93
home businesses 81, 94, 123
homework 76, 119
hoplink 13, 138
host 48, 125, 158
hubpages 65, 85
hubs 65, 85

I

Inc 53, 68-9, 72, 74, 128
incentive 108, 128, 158
income 29, 33, 35, 42, 45-6, 48, 53-4, 56-8, 60, 64-5, 68, 78, 80, 82, 102-3, 134-5 [14]
  living 24-5
  massive internet 94
  monthly 14, 46, 57, 140
  passive 44-5, 47, 51, 58, 184
  source of 62, 183
income online 95, 132-3
  handsome 60
  monthly 60
income opportunities 53, 95

Increase Affiliate Sales 128
Increase Affiliate Sales Overnight 9
individuals 19, 40, 44, 110, 145-6, 178
industry 18, 33, 35, 70, 111, 146, 162, 180-1
industry workings 95
info 5, 43
Information Visit Wealthy Affiliate Review 166-7, 171, 177, 179
Instant Cash Affiliate Programs 10, 159-60
Instant Cash Affiliate Programs and Instant Commission Affiliate Programs 159
instant commission affiliate programs 159-60
internet 6-7, 15-19, 21-4, 35, 37, 44-6, 53, 57-8, 77, 87, 96-8, 109-10, 119-21, 134-5, 141-2, 161-3 [16]
  projected annual 179
Internet Affiliate 6, 19-20
internet affiliate income 51
internet affiliate marketing 58, 136, 165-6, 170-1, 176, 178
internet age 73
internet basics 93
internet business 9, 64, 122-4, 131, 141
Internet Business Entrepreneur building 64
internet business matching services, comprehensive 70
Internet Businesses, multiple 64
internet coach 69
internet connection 36, 44, 154, 172
internet economy 120
internet entrepreneur 19, 182
internet experience 171
Internet Gurus 19
internet home jobs 6, 24-5
internet hosting 43
internet job 24
  perfect home 24
internet landscape 119
internet market 82
internet marketers 23, 52, 70, 153, 166
  wealthy 75
internet marketing 7, 10, 23-4, 29, 69, 75-6, 81, 89, 98, 112-14, 117-18, 137-8, 146, 150-2, 154-5, 179-82 [3]
  free 98
internet-marketing-2009 71
Internet Marketing Business 110
internet marketing careers 150
internet marketing coach 69
internet marketing education 184
internet marketing field 139
internet marketing mentors 70
internet marketing online business 48
internet marketing pro-gram 135
internet marketing site 139

internet marketing strategies 183-4
  popular 183
internet marketing success 97
internet marketing techniques 146, 182
Internet Marketing University 180
internet marketing world 111
internet mentor 70
internet millionaire 96
Internet of software products 45
internet platform opportunities 184
internet resources 135
internet site 43-4
internet spending 170, 176-8
internet traffic 146
internet transactions 134
internet wealth 19, 96-7

J
Jack 44
jobs 24, 35, 48, 53, 59, 61-3, 76, 82, 91, 96, 113-14, 117-18, 130-1, 145, 170-1, 176 [8]
Joint ventures 126, 129
jump 79-80, 137, 154, 163, 182
JV partner 126-7
JV partnership 126

K
karma 69
Key Steps to Affiliate Marketing Success 6, 38
Key Strategies to Making Money On-line 36
Key Strategies to Making Money Online 6
keywords 39, 52, 67, 85, 94, 103, 109, 130, 175
Kimberlyn 185
knowledge 34, 52-3, 58, 70, 131, 167, 170, 172, 175, 182
Kyle 148-9

L
landing page 85, 93, 104, 150, 156, 175
learning 62, 83, 92, 112, 122, 130, 133, 138, 162, 166, 175, 180
lets 27, 31, 62, 141
leverage 76, 83, 131, 168-70
liability 3
life 21, 30, 37, 46, 49, 51, 55-6, 58, 72, 86, 135, 144, 173
links 13, 15, 19, 30, 34, 36-7, 39, 52, 57, 64-7, 75-6, 83-7, 106, 153-5, 157-8, 169 [10]
  referral 66-7
  sponsored 20
list 27, 40, 67, 72, 78, 94, 109, 118, 138, 168
living online, good 11, 166-7
loads 27, 106

Lone Ranger 139-40
long-term success 162-3

M
Make Extra Money 11, 171
Make Money 6-7, 11, 13, 19, 21, 58, 125, 178
Make Money During 11, 165
Make Money on Internet 6, 44
Make Money Online 9, 96, 124
Make Money Online During 11, 176
make money online methods 156
Make Money Online on Autopilot 9, 131
Make Money Surfing 6, 15
Make-Money-Systems.net 135
make-money-visitbank.com 46
make money with google products 153
make-online-money-fast.com 111
Make-Online-Money-Fast.com 111
Making Fast Money Online 10, 159
making money online 6, 55, 74, 76, 90, 120-2, 131-3, 136-7, 174
market 13-15, 27-8, 33, 35, 42, 55, 57-8, 69-70, 74-5, 77, 83, 125-6, 160-1, 167-8, 178-9, 183 [9]
market affiliate products 13
marketers 13, 33, 46, 83, 111, 162-3, 177
  best affiliate 161
  determined affiliate 167
  expert affiliate 108
  internet affiliate 171
  newbie affiliate 182
  successful affiliate 162
marketing 6, 15, 21, 27, 29, 31, 36, 43, 98, 112, 116, 125, 127, 130, 134, 162-4 [4]
marketing campaign, viral 40, 84
marketing efforts, casino affiliate 115
marketing opportunities, research affiliate 123
marketing products, released high quality affiliate 111
marketing programs
  online affiliate 10, 164-5
  time affiliate 120
marketing tools 27, 70
marketplaces, giant affiliate 158
master 93-4, 125, 133, 181
Matt's website 125
Maverick Money Maker program 141
Maverick Money Makers 10, 14, 16, 89, 139
members 45, 82, 101, 104, 140, 180
mentor 7, 69-70, 145, 185
merchants 13-14, 25, 35, 68-9, 71-2, 123, 157, 167
minded work 82
mindset 9, 136-7

mistakes 69, 87, 99, 169, 172, 182
models 37, 86, 162
  popular affiliate marketing business 36
Modules of Affiliate Funnel System 112
money 16-17, 21-3, 27-30, 33, 35-7, 44-6, 53-6, 62-5, 72-3, 76-8, 80-2, 86-9, 95-7, 118-24, 133-7, 163-8 [25]
  days 140
  decent amount of 124, 163
  easy 8, 26-7, 109, 134
  exceptional 87
  extra 23, 70, 172
  free 131
  hard earned 110
  involved 173
  lose 37, 42
  making 7, 15, 17, 19, 34, 36, 53, 55, 61, 109, 112, 119, 131, 137, 160-1, 174 [1]
  online 14, 16
  spending 22
  start earning 38, 41, 86
  throwing 83
money brokering 27
money idea 26
money maker 16
Money Making Machine 11, 173
money-making opportunities 143
Money Making Review 71
Money Making System 38, 41, 86
money on-line 28, 151
money online 7, 9-10, 19, 23, 25, 28, 34, 59, 98-9, 113-14, 119, 125, 154-7, 160-1, 163-7, 173-4 [13]
  fast 159
  how to make 153
  how to Make 96
  started making 79
  track 174
money online programs 90
money online sector 29
money surfing 15-16
money wave 109
month, first 162-3
Most affiliate companies 14
Most affiliate programs 15
multi-level marketing MLM 26
multimillion dollar businesses 184
Murder 117-18, 152, 155
mymlmmagic.info 19

N
name 32, 43-4, 75, 81-2, 94, 114, 148, 158, 162

network 10, 15, 71-2, 115, 117, 123, 160, 165
affiliate marketing online 160
network marketing 26
New business owners 127
New Internet Economy 9, 120
Newbie Workbook 89-90
Newbie Workbook Review 8, 89
newbies 14, 29-30
newspapers 94, 143-4
niche 26-7, 41, 54, 67, 78, 93-4, 102, 109, 112, 122, 125, 131, 150, 153, 156, 181
niche market 93-4, 109, 122, 175
niche marketing 122, 160
Nightingale-Conant organization 145
nutshell 53

O
offline business 42
on-line business 31
one-tier 26
online 1, 9, 13-14, 16, 22, 32, 34-5, 48, 53-4, 64, 68, 72, 142-3, 170-3, 176, 181-2 [5]
online affiliate 29
online affiliate business 102
Online Affiliate Marketing 149
online affiliate marketing business 164
online Affiliate Marketing University 35
online affiliate pro-gram 145
online affiliate training 34-5
right 35
online business 60, 91, 95-6, 101, 114, 164, 184
profitable 69, 149
online business owners 97
online business profile 70
online commerce 162-3
online income streams 66
Online Income System 8, 90-1, 99-100, 112
online marketer 34, 53, 68-9, 72, 74, 97
online marketing 105, 109, 127, 133, 148
Online Millionaire 38, 41, 86
online retailers 25-6
online sales 95
online salespeople 95
online school 23
ORDER Maverick Money Makers 141
organization 47, 77
outsource 132-3
overnight 9, 90, 117-18
ow-to-cloak-your-affiliate-links 106
owner, retired business 44

P

part-time job 110-11
parties 126
partner 66, 126-8
  potential joint venture 127
passion 34, 55, 146, 153, 159-60
passionate 159
passive income streams 49, 56, 59
patient 98, 153
pay-per-visit 175
payment processing 107
payments 32, 42, 45, 64, 72, 134, 138-9
PayPal account 159-60, 179
pennies 14, 121, 142
People Time & Money 85
people's work 52
person 3, 28, 39, 44, 68-9, 74, 84, 89, 96, 98, 113, 121, 126, 128, 135, 167 [3]
personal custom website 124
personal site 77
personal website 47, 49, 56
personalized embedded links 149
phrase 26, 96
plan 8, 16-17, 70, 90-1, 100, 115, 181
Plug-In Profit Site 116
popularity 45, 75, 81, 120, 146-7
post 40, 52, 63, 67, 76, 116, 120
  forum 63
post affiliate links 85
posting 30, 36, 55, 76, 115
ppc 14, 97
PPC 8, 22, 37, 76, 96-7, 166, 171, 176, 179
PPC ads 115
press 70, 99
Press Releases 85-6, 94
price 25, 27, 60, 65, 74, 101, 143-4, 156, 183
problem 19, 33, 37, 41, 48, 50, 62, 66, 73, 77, 86, 103, 109, 126, 128-30, 157-8 [3]
process 40, 91, 109, 112, 121, 140, 147, 156, 161, 163-4
Proctor, Bob 10, 144-5
product website 19, 31
Productivity Epiphany 47, 49, 51, 56, 58-60
profile, lower 25-6
profitable home online job 24
profits 6, 13, 16-17, 27, 34, 58, 60, 64, 68, 89-90, 106-7, 112, 119-20, 123, 126-8, 168 [4]
program CDNOW 25-6
programs online, selling affiliate 124
promises 127, 141, 166

promotions 13, 116-18, 125, 146, 156
prospect 43, 88, 93
publisher 3, 71-2, 147-8
Publishers Join Affiliate Net-works 71
Publishers Join Affiliate Networks 7
purchase 20, 48, 54, 60, 62-4, 102, 104, 110, 113, 123, 125, 128-9, 138, 145-6, 158-9

Q
quit 22, 51, 61-2, 100, 113-14, 167

R
rank 36, 125, 145
recession 7, 11, 48, 165, 170, 176, 178
recession cycle 11, 178-9
recession graph, downward 11, 170
recession trends 11, 176-7
Referral programs 15, 26
referrals 15, 44, 52, 66-7, 101-2
referring paying customers 62-3
register 13, 15, 54, 67, 104
relationship 50, 94, 118, 133
reputation 126-7, 139
residual income 8, 76-7, 81-2
residual income business opportunities 18
Residual Income Using Affiliate Programs 7, 76
resource boxes 36, 65, 83-4
resources 23-4, 84, 94, 103, 131, 169-70
revenue 34, 66, 68, 85, 95, 120, 148
revenue stream 68-9
REVIEW Maverick Money Makers 140
Review Sites 16, 37, 39
reviewthewealthyaffiliate.blogspot.com 151, 172
Richard 146
Right Affiliate Products 8, 102
RIGHT NOW 109
ringtone websites 21
  popular 20
ringtones 20-1
risks 42, 106, 183-4
Ryan, Peter 53, 68-9, 72, 74

S
safety, worker 134
salary 176-7
sales 13-14, 31, 43, 57, 77-8, 93-5, 101-2, 104-5, 108, 115-16, 127-8, 155-6, 158, 166-7, 171, 176-7 [18]
  extended 26
sales copy 75, 103-4
sales funnel 107

sales letters 30, 108
sales page 30, 90, 138, 150, 153
sales pitches 67, 125, 180
scams 9, 87, 97, 111-12, 134-5, 165-6
scenario 68, 91
search engines 15, 17, 20, 22, 26, 34, 38-9, 67, 76, 84, 101, 109, 115, 130, 157, 174
seat 46
secret affiliate weapon 31-2
Secret to Affiliate Marketing 8
Secret to Affiliate Marketing Part 109
secrets 20, 36, 141, 150
Secrets to Make Money Promoting 6, 19
selection 15, 183
self-sabotage 50-1
SEO 39, 130, 157, 176
services 3, 42-3, 52, 60-3, 65-6, 68, 70, 72, 79, 84, 101, 115, 124, 127, 159-60, 164 [7]
set 13, 37-8, 41, 52, 68, 73, 84, 86, 89, 93-5, 123-4, 132, 144, 167, 175, 178 [1]
shady internet work opportunities 134
shopping 123-4
sign 66, 69-71, 75, 80, 95, 100, 107, 116, 142, 146, 150, 158, 163, 165
site 15-16, 26-8, 36-7, 39-41, 43-4, 62-3, 68, 71-3, 87, 102, 105-6, 109, 114-15, 148-9, 156-8, 168 [10]
skill 83, 133, 144, 179, 181
social marketing 40
Social Marketing Traffic 83
software 13, 27, 35, 96, 101, 129, 174, 181
sounds 42-3, 55, 75-6, 120
source 76, 95, 99, 109, 169
speakers, public 7, 64, 66
squeeze page 29, 65, 78
Squidoo 65, 83, 85
Squidoo.com 37-8
step guide 120-2
steps 6, 11, 15, 25, 35, 90, 92, 94, 99-100, 109-10, 120-2, 127, 140, 142, 163, 168
Steps to Internet Marketing 10, 152
strength 99, 145, 152
subject 33, 52, 63, 67, 73, 78, 163, 175, 178
submissions 115
subscribers 118
Super Affiliate Business Home Business Model 94
Super Affiliate Home Business Model 8, 93
super affiliate status 93
system 33, 46, 91-2, 111-12, 120, 145, 158, 185
  tracking 102, 158

T

Tan, Fabian 117-18, 152, 155
teach 14, 16, 22, 70, 80, 89-90, 129, 137, 149, 154, 180
affiliate marketing courses 112
teams 140, 146, 185
techniques 19, 21, 70, 98, 111, 122, 141, 147, 149, 162, 176
affiliate traffic generation 80
terms 48, 50, 58-9, 70, 72, 81, 87, 98, 121, 137-8, 156
theonlinemoneysecret.com 34, 120-2, 161, 163-5
tier 27, 69, 145-6
tier affiliate pro-gram 26
tier programs 25-6, 77
Tiers of Affiliate Marketing 9, 121
time income 19, 53, 130
tips 1, 5-6, 9, 16, 42, 79, 84-5, 116, 122, 149, 177
Tips and Advice on Affiliate Revenue 1
Tips on Affiliate Referrals 7, 51
title 39, 67
tons 80, 95, 118, 153, 169, 180
tools 69-70, 72, 85, 91, 103, 109, 124, 168, 180-1
top 10, 19, 67, 70, 78, 90, 93, 97-8, 158, 160
topic 35, 39, 52, 60, 73, 93, 109, 182
complex 122
trackback 52
trade 136, 168, 181
trademarks 3
traffic 8, 21, 28, 31, 38-40, 43, 45, 68, 73, 76-7, 82-3, 85-6, 116-17, 125, 130, 156-7 [8]
free 14, 153
generating 38, 117
incoming 52
traffic/sales 95
training, best affiliate 35, 181
trends 119, 123-4, 164
monitor Internet 161
trial, free 20, 89, 91, 100
tricks 79, 113, 122, 168
trivial 119
trust 52, 54, 67, 127, 151
Try Free Affiliate Marketing 8, 96
tutorials 35, 110, 151, 172, 180-1
Twitter 40, 83
two-tier 26
two-tier marketing 68-9
two-tier programs 26

U
ugly 67, 106, 157
update 36, 54
usage 146-7
users 22, 36, 40, 68, 72, 161

Using Affiliate Programs to Make Money Online 9, 124

V
vendor 64-5, 72
video marketing 132
videos 35, 70, 132, 142, 180-1
Vince 47, 49, 51, 56, 58-9
Viral marketing 40, 132
Viral Marketing 40, 84, 132
visitbank 13, 77, 153
Visitbank 6, 13, 30-1, 44-6, 58, 60, 74-5, 78-9, 107, 138-9, 150
Visitbank Affiliate 7, 59
visitbank ID 75
visitbank products 7, 45, 58, 79-80
Visitbank Profit Guide 9, 137
visitbank profits 10, 150-1
visitors 14, 27, 37, 39, 43, 64, 75, 101-2, 104-5, 114-16, 118-19, 125, 130-1, 146-8, 156-7, 168 [2]
  unique 117, 152, 155

W
Ways to Make Money During 11, 165
wealth 7, 55, 134, 138
  psychology of 55-6
Wealthy Affiliate 10, 22, 24, 110-11, 148-51, 172
Wealthy Affiliate Review 172
Wealthy Affiliate University 35, 180-1
web 33, 36-7, 97-8, 121, 174
web site 81-2, 96, 121, 130-1
web surfers 115
webpages 17, 64-6
website 15-17, 20-5, 28-30, 33-4, 38-9, 44-6, 53-4, 66, 73, 84-5, 113, 124-5, 127-8, 144-5, 147-8, 155-6 [23]
  advertising 166
  company 155
  high-traffic 144
  legitimate 110
  multiple 77
  non-adult 25-6
website builder 181
website copy 93
website creation 14, 133, 171
website development 179
website hosting 77
website link 84
website maker 17
website owner 27, 113, 134
website syndication 25-6
Website Using Chitika 6, 16
website's ranking 157

weight loss 143
Widget Affiliate Offer Review 67
wisdom 56, 58-9, 175
work 14, 23, 32-3, 43-4, 50-2, 61-3, 77, 87-8, 91-2, 99-101, 126-7, 129-30, 132-3, 142-3, 168-70, 184-5 [19]
work-from-home opportunities 134
work online 82, 171
worker, common 99
workforce, real 53
Working Online 11, 170
workings, inner 180
would-be internet entrepreneurs 170, 176
WS domain names 81-2
www.affiliateavalanche.com 144
www.affiliateconquerer.com/coaching 80, 137, 154
www.affiliatefuel.info 129
www.currencymoneycash.com 92, 100
www.ExplosiveTrafficSystem.com 117, 119, 152, 155
www.hasoffers.com 53, 68-9, 72, 74
www.HomeBusiness.us 116
www.homeonlinejobs.net 25
www.InstantMaverickMoneyMaker.com 133
www.internetmarketingstrategypro.com 139
www.livelifetothefullest.biz 125
www.Make-Money-At-HomeNow.com 38, 41, 86
www.makeextramoneyonline.org 114
www.makehomebusiness.com 63-4
www.marketingrichman.com 146
www.massiveautopilotincome.com 168-70
www.maverickmoneymakerssecretclub.com 71
www.money-online.tv 175
www.moneymakingideaonline.info/L6 66
www.moneymakingideaonline.info/Speakers 66
www.MurderYourJob.com 117-18, 152, 155
www.PeaceOfMindMoney.com 47, 49, 51, 56, 58-60
www.profitlancereview.org 105
www.super-affiliate-tools.com 178
www.Top3ProvenOnlineMoneyMakers.com 87
www.truemaverickmoneymaker.com 76
www.VinceHarris.com 47, 49, 51, 56, 60
www.wealthyaffiliate-reviewer.com 166-7, 171, 177, 179
www.wealthyaffiliatesnow.info 22
www.WebsicknessRx.com 21
www.wpeasyads.com 42

Y

Yahoo 8, 96-7, 153
year cookie 27

Printed in the United States
150161LV00001B/104/P

9 781921 644078